D1234202

Fulfilling the Dream

*My Path to Leadership
and Finding Purpose
Through Serving Others*

Fulfilling the Dream

My Path to Leadership and Finding Purpose Through Serving Others

WAYMAN BRITT
with Ray Serafin

First published in the United States
by WBE Books

WBE BOOKS

A division of Wayman Britt Enterprises, LLC
P.O. Box 7, Ada, MI 49301
info@wbebooks.com | www.wbebooks.com

For information about this book, contact the publisher
at the above address or (email, website addresses)

Information about special bulk quantity sales to
qualified institutions and organizations are available
from the publisher at the above addresses

979-8-9856123-0-1 this edition
979-8-9856123-1-8 ebook
979-8-9856123-2-5 audiobook

Cover, dust jacket, photo section, and text design by Jacinta Calcut
Image Graphics & Design
image-gd.com

Printed in the United States of America
by Sheridan MI
Chelsea, Michigan

DEDICATION

To my wife Dinah,
my faithful companion and friend.
Thanks for helping to keep the fire burning in me
and helping me to soar.

To my children and grandchildren
who give me hope for the future.

And to my mom and dad,
Oscar and Mamie Britt,
for your love, grit and determination
that still live in me today.

CHAPTER 1

Our Vast Potential

My first-ever paycheck came from buffing and shining floors in the Health Department and Prosecutor's Office in Michigan's Genesee County Administration Building. As a student at Flint Northern High School, I was glad to have a few bucks in my pocket without having to ask Ma and Daddy for money. Cleaning surfaces may not have been a prestigious job, but I took pride in giving those floors a deep clean. I could not imagine that one day I would work in another county office on the other side of the state. But in 2018, I was officially appointed administrator/controller of Michigan's fourth-largest county.

I grew up in North Carolina during a time when segregation was strictly enforced. We were farmers and struggled to make ends meet. I traveled a lengthy and twisting path to become the first African American to be named to the top executive post in Kent County, which has a population of about 650,000 people and a budget of $500 million.

As a young boy, my first glimpse of a brighter future occurred when I went away to a Boy Scouts camp. I began to think of a better life. My hopes were the essence of the American Dream, which is based on a belief that anyone can achieve their own version of success through sacrifice and hard work.

I didn't always know the path that life would carry me, but I was willing to put in the effort.

In pursuing my dreams, I came to realize that the opportunities for upward mobility were not equal for everyone. In his famous "I Have a Dream" speech, Martin Luther King Jr. recognized that America has not always lived up to its promise that "all men are created equal." But he insisted that the ideal of equal opportunity was enshrined in the country's founding principles and that it was time for America to make good on its promise. As I rose through leadership ranks with the aid of others, I committed myself to helping young people fulfill their own dreams. I sought to clear away the personal and systemic impediments that put many people at a disadvantage from the time they are born.

When I was in the fourth grade, my teacher Mrs. Thelma Wall said to me that I would be a leader. I didn't understand what she saw in me, but she must have recognized some underlying potential. I still needed to learn many lessons on the way to attaining a leadership position. From my parents, I absorbed bedrock principles like a work ethic and the importance of treating everyone with respect. Playing basketball, I discovered ways to relate to people in order to harness the power of teamwork. During a nearly quarter-century of work at office furniture manufacturer Steelcase, I honed the skills needed to empower people and give them the tools and the knowledge to succeed. And it was in this period that I found a deeper understanding of the inclusive and empowering mindset needed to move a community forward.

My journey is a story of learning to lead at every step while overcoming discrimination and other challenges to become a groundbreaker. It is also a tale of faith that God wanted me to achieve my full potential by becoming someone who served others and helped them to grab hold of their own destiny.

One summer while I was a member of the University of Michigan basketball team, I had a wonderful experience playing a pickup game with NBA star George "The Iceman" Gervin. It was so cool. We ran the fast break better than I had ever run it and afterwards, he gave me a pair of his Nike shoes to wear. When practice began that season at Michigan I shared with an assistant coach that I wanted to be as good as George Gervin and pattern my game after him. The assistant coach scoffed, and told me I'd never be like George.

In spite of what he said, I believed in myself. That season I became a better player and helped the team reach the NCAA Mideast regional finals in Tuscaloosa, Alabama, where we knocked off the top-seeded Notre Dame squad who had just snapped UCLA's record 88-game winning streak. Two years later, I served as captain of the team and we went all the way to the NCAA finals. I made a mark, even though I was only 6"1¾", unusually short for playing forward.

In my view, the greatest tragedy in life is not death, but a life that fails to fulfill its purpose and potential. Far too many people start with dreams and ideas that end up dying on the vine, shriveling up and never fulfilled. Belief in yourself is essential. My experience taught me that you should never let anyone superimpose their thoughts upon you. You must be willing to fight through the tough times and trust that you have an important part to play in this world.

Setbacks threaten to shake confidence in our abilities, and disappointments certainly tested my mettle. I hoped for a prolonged career in the NBA, but didn't make it with the Los Angeles Lakers and Detroit Pistons. I went through personal issues in life that were difficult to get through. But I gained strength from the experience of overcoming adversity. These setbacks turned out to be steps on the way to understanding my true potential and the obligation I had to use my abilities to help others.

Most of us will not be an Albert Einstein, with our name and accomplishments remembered forever in the history books. But that does not lessen our need to create some meaning in our lives, to have our thoughts and actions live on after us, to be remembered in some way. The world isn't connected by molecules. It's connected by stories, traditions, memories, hopes, and dreams. I want to leave something on this earth and I want it to be a story that reflects the many lessons I learned.

Where do you think it's best to plant a young tree – a clearing in an old-growth forest or an open field? Ecologists tell us that a young tree grows better when it's planted in an area with older trees. The reason, it seems, is that the roots of the young tree are able to follow the pathways created by former trees and implant themselves more deeply. Over time, the roots of many trees may actually graft themselves to one another, creating an intricate, interdependent foundation hidden under the ground. In this way, stronger trees share resources with weaker ones so that the whole forest becomes healthier. That's why legacy is important. It is a connection across time, with a need for those who have come before us and a responsibility to those who come after us.

As an African American, I have encountered both overt and covert racism. There were times I wanted to leave a situation because I could tell that some people resented me or wanted to block my ambitions. But I stuck it out in hopes of making a difference. I hope my perseverance helps motivate disadvantaged young people to aspire to be leaders. And I wish to give them an inside scoop on what it takes to overcome the obstacles they will encounter.

We're at a crossroads as a nation. How do we create an environment for all to fulfill their dreams, versus some? The way we answer this question will determine the future growth and prosperity of our country. I have come to realize that systems matter. Systemic racism is often unconscious. Its products are inequities in areas such as housing, education, health care, hiring processes and law enforcement.

I don't bring up racism in an attempt to point fingers at anyone. That is simply not productive. I believe I can be more effective by developing relationships with leaders in business, in health care, in community groups and in government. These are important influencers, and I seek to raise their awareness of how inequalities have a negative effect on everyone. We need to work collaboratively to change the way things are. The rabid partisanship we see today won't get us where we want to go.

When I determined that my mission in life is to serve others, I analyzed how I could best do that. I concluded that serving others is more than giving people things. It's first of all about what I could do to better myself so I could be of value to other people. That way I became an asset to other people, so they could capitalize on the experience, knowledge and the social capital I bring to the table. Jesus was the greatest at inspiring others to be the best they can be and gave us a powerful example of how someone can lead by serving others. You can move mountains when you learn to perfect serving and empowering others.

I believe there is greatness in all of us. My life is evidence for how you can grab hold of destiny if you're willing to fight through the tough times and believe that you can help make the world a better place. If I had allowed some of the obstacles to conquer me, I would never have stayed the course long enough for better things to materialize. Potential is meant to be released, to be used to benefit the world, not wasted. Some people have thousands of reasons why they cannot do what they want to, when all they need is one reason why they can.

One of my favorite movies is "Secretariat." It's about the horse that won the Triple Crown and in fact broke records at each of the three tracks and won his final race by an astonishing 31 lengths. He is still regarded as the greatest racehorse of all time.

When Penny, the owner, first showed Secretariat to her father, he said to her, "Let him run his race." Along the way, Penny learned to run her own race while letting her horse do the same. None of us will ever know what we can accomplish unless we go all in and run our race. As I write this, I still have some gas in the tank. I continue to run my race, focusing on serving others.

I hope the story of how I have run my race will encourage others to courageously and confidently run their own races.

·- CHAPTER 2 -·

Growing Up on Tobacco Road

I grew up in a rusty shack
All I owned was hangin' on my back
The Lord knows, how I loathe
This place called Tobacco Road
But it's a home, yeah
The only life I'll ever know

These were lyrics from a hit record by Lou Rawls when I was a boy growing up in Smithfield, North Carolina. *Tobacco Road* was also the title of an earlier Erskine Caldwell novel about poor tenant farmers during the Depression. That's how the notion of Tobacco Road became a symbol of poverty-stricken rural areas in the southern states where tobacco is grown. And North Carolina grows more tobacco than any other state.

You won't find this road on a map of Smithfield, but the term describes my family's existence at that time. However, unlike the line in the song, it would not be "the only life I'll ever know." Instead, it was just the beginning of a thrilling journey that I could scarcely imagine during my first few years on this earth.

I was born in 1954 in Wilson's Mills, North Carolina, the seventh of nine children of Oscar and Mamie Britt. My siblings and I referred to them as "Daddy" and "Ma." I remember mostly living in a three-room house at the end of a long dirt road in Smithfield Township, which is 31 miles southeast of Raleigh and 106 miles northwest of Wilmington, where Michael Jordan grew up. My family home had electric lights, but that was about it for the comforts that Americans take for granted today. As many as three of us slept in a bed, with three brothers and two sisters in the same bedroom.

The house lacked running water, so we drew what we needed from a well for drinking, bathing, cooking and laundry. We had to take turns fetching water with a pulley and chain from the well. The bucket would often leak and we would have to replace it every year or so because it would rust out. During winter months, the water might freeze in the pail in our kitchen. We heated the home with wood that we cut down and would bring in from the woodpile near the well. We would load the wood in the potbelly stove that provided heat for the rooms. The house had electricity, so we warmed water for cooking and bathing on our electric stove, pouring it into a large metal tub for our baths. And without running water, we had to use an outhouse, which was an especially unpleasant adventure in the dark of night.

Swift Creek was at the back of our house. It connected to the Neuse River just outside the City of Smithfield, and would often overflow during heavy rains in the spring and on occasion in late summer when it was hurricane season. Sometimes it would overflow like a lake right up to our home. But we would have some fun when the creek overflowed during a cold snap by taking a rocking chair outside our house and pulling each other with a rope across the ice.

Most of the families in the small city of Smithfield had running water. My life was rugged living out in the township —the "country"—but not depressing. Even though we didn't have a lot, I never had the feeling we lived in poverty. Later, when I started liking girls, I realized I had a disadvantage against the boys who dressed nicely or had a nice car.

We were sharecropper farmers, primarily raising tobacco and cotton as cash crops, while also planting vegetables. Share-cropping is a system in which the landowner provides the land and often leases equipment to the tenants who contribute the labor. Sharecroppers keep what is left after they are able to pay back the owners. Weather patterns or low market prices can diminish profits, making economic insecurity a fact of life for sharecroppers. I never knew what the arrangement was with Daddy. I just know that it always seemed that he could never get ahead and that he had to always make side hustles selling a few vegetable crops, chopping wood and working in a hog slaughterhouse in the winter. We grew cucumbers, watermelon, cantaloupe, sweet potatoes, white potatoes, peanuts, corn, sweet peas, butter beans, green beans, tomatoes, cabbage, okra and collard greens for our family consumption while also taking some to market. We also sold pears from the tree in the front yard when the fruit was plentiful. But tobacco and cotton were king and queen.

When I say "we were farmers," I mean the whole family, including the six boys and three girls. In order of birth, the kids were Myrtle (we called her Mert); Alonza; Kinnie (whom we called Ray); Jimmie; Jean; James (aka Curt); me; Jay (Jay Bird, as we called him); and Joyce. My older brothers and cousins affectionately referred to me as "Moon" because I had a round face that reminded them of a full moon. My grandpa John would pinch my cheeks and say, "Let me see those cheeks, boy." At the time of my writing this book, both of my parents, my sisters Mert, Jean and Joyce, and brother Ray are all deceased.

Yes, we were poor. There is a stereotype that poverty is the result of laziness, but nothing could be further from the truth. We worked hard. Large, industrialized farms are more common now in tobacco-leaf growing areas. But in my youth, small-scale family farms were the norm and it was hard to scrape out a living. It's estimated that 500,000 barns used for curing tobacco dotted the North Carolina countryside during the 1950s.

Our farm consisted of about 75 acres. Many days, the members of my family were busy from sunup to sundown. Like my brothers and sisters, I would sometimes get up as early as 3 or 4 in the morning to do farm work, then go to school from 7 a.m. to 3 p.m., and come home to work some more on the farm.

A majority of the work to grow, harvest and process tobacco for market was done by hand. We grew seedlings in the late winter, planted them into a field in the spring, and removed weeds and pests as they grew. About late July or early August—the time that summer reached its hottest temperatures—it was time to begin harvesting, a process that was very physically demanding.

The big tobacco leaves start ripening from the bottom, so we began by plucking the row of leaves closest to the ground. A week later we would go back to the next row and do the same, and so forth for several weeks. After collecting leaves, we would bring them back to the area of the curing barn, tie leaves into stalks and then loop them around sticks. Several bundles of leaves would go on each stick, which was about 4-feet long. Then we would hang the sticks overhead, about eight rows going all the way up to the top of the curing barn.

We used kerosene heaters for the curing process, an essential step in the aging procedure to receive the best prices at auction. It would take several days to get the juice out of the green leaves and cured. When the tobacco had dried, we would strip the leaves off of the sticks and bundled the leaves together to go to market for auction.

Cotton was another crop that grew well in the long, hot summers. Picking cotton would beat your hands to death as you pulled the lint from the sharp end of the boil. We would put the cotton in burlap sacks, and by the time my sib-

Picking tobacco leaves was hard work when I grew up before mechanization.

lings and I were about 10 or 11 years old, we were expected to collect 100 pounds a day.

Daddy was a taskmaster, and he really pushed us. He had to, because it was always a struggle to make ends meet. He was one of the best farmers around, with beautiful crops. He would shoot small game like rabbits and squirrels and we skinned and gutted them for meat.

Yet he was always in debt to the boss men—the guys that owned the property and the equipment he was leasing. He had to give most of our hard-earned money to them. He would buy everything on credit at the grocery and the feed store, but he could never get ahead. To supplement our diets, we got government cheese—blocks of cheese that the government bought to prop up dairy prices and then distribute to poor people. Daddy had big responsibilities, and it weighed on him. He never smiled. He had no high hopes that his kids would go on to succeed at something else, figuring we were all meant to work on a farm.

But he gave me an edge, an attitude of working hard. Daddy would not tolerate excuses. One afternoon, after getting home from school I was tired and hardly standing up, beginning to fall asleep as I was separating tobacco from sticks. He took a stick, whacked me on my butt and yelled at me: "What the hell is wrong with you, boy? You better wake up," he said.

Ma also worked relentlessly. She got up in the morning and cooked breakfast, then went to work in the fields or would wash all our clothes. She cooked dinner—which we now call lunch—then it was back to work until it was time to fix supper. She also was deeply spiritual, and this led her to be a loving, caring person. She instilled in me the notion that I should always treat people right. Always respect others, especially your elders, she reminded me. This was counsel that has remained with me my entire life.

Ma was only 66 years old when she passed away. The only possession of hers that I took after her funeral was a poster. It said: "Love is like a butterfly. It goes wherever it pleases, and it pleases wherever it goes." That was the epitome of Ma. She had a caring heart and truly loved people.

My sister Mert, born 13 years before me, taught me my ABCs before I was old enough to go to school. I was a scared little kid and she helped me get out of my shell. I had no idea what school was like until she took me to high school with her when I was about five years old. She drove the school bus and I was able to ride in it, and then sit in the room with the juniors and seniors of Smithfield's Johnston County Training School. This was a big deal, as it gave me a chance to find out what school life was like ahead of time. I was lucky that my brothers and sisters helped me get over my anxiety about going to school.

I entered first grade at Short Journey, an all-Black, segregated school in Smithfield Township. This was still the Jim Crow era in the southern United States. Jim Crow laws were designed to maintain an old social order in which African Americans were regarded as second-class citizens. Various schemes such as poll taxes and ridiculously hard literacy tests were used to prevent Black citizens from voting. Racial segregation was enforced for schools, restrooms, buses and other aspects of everyday life. Drinking fountains were separated by signs that read "Whites Only" and "Colored." Even cemeteries were segregated.

I had my first up-close encounter with open racism just before I started grade school. A school bus with White kids passed me and started yelling. One kid pointed a finger at me and shouted, "Nigger!" I asked Ma, "What was he saying?" She replied, "Oh, don't worry about that." She didn't really tell me what it was about. Looking back, I think she was trying to shield me from the hurt for as long as she could. And I feel she was hoping I would learn to brush off opinions based on ignorant prejudice.

All of the teachers at Short Journey School were Black, as was the principal, Mrs. Eva Cooper. They were good to us and gave us a great foundation, intellectually and artistically. The

Supreme Court had not yet banned prayer in public schools, and every day we had a devotional exercise. I remember being in the room where we did the devotional, and the way the sun came beaming in from the big atrium on the left. Right up at the front of the stage were words from Shakespeare: "To thine own self be true." As I grew older, I remembered this quote and took it to mean that I ought to be true to my dream and purpose in life. I should find a purpose in life and commit myself to making the most of any God-given talent. Mahatma Gandhi said, "The best way to find yourself is to lose yourself in the service of others." I also believe in the admonition from the Bible, that "To whom much is given, much will be required."

At Short Journey, the teachers really pushed the arts programs. Mrs. Fuller emphasized the fine arts, including drama and music. Her class inspired me to begin singing. I later joined the choir and became a part of the drama club at Flint Northern High School in Michigan. As an adult, I became the choir director at St. Philip's Episcopal Church in Grand Rapids, where we turned the solemn, quiet little congregation into a group that became known for the kind of spiritual gospel music that I was brought up on. I believe music is an essential part of being human. People who practice music therapy understand that it can help us cope with our emotional and social needs. But no matter your situation, music has the power to enrich your life.

Some songs have stuck in my head for many years. One that I first sang as a youngster at Short Journey School was Frank Sinatra's rendition of "My Way." It had a beautiful melody, and its words reinforced Shakespeare's advice of "To thine own self be true." The song was about believing in yourself, and it got engrained in my attitude. "My Way" captures the spirit of loving life and a willingness to take on any challenge, with lyrics like:

I've lived, a life that's full
I traveled each and every highway
And more, much more than this
I did it my way.

The first film I ever saw at a movie theatre was "The Sound of Music," and the catchy tunes from that story have also stuck with me. The movie starred Julie Andrews and Christopher Plummer in a story about a music-loving Austrian family that escaped the Nazis. It was hugely popular and won the 1965 Oscar for best picture. The beautiful mountain scenery opened my eyes to a whole different world. That put a mark on me, allowing me to see more possibilities for life.

I saw "The Sound of Music" sitting in the balcony of the only movie theatre in downtown Smithfield. I wondered why all of the Black kids were sitting up there, and the White kids were on the ground floor. Later, when I studied the history of African Americans, I realized that this was another example of Jim Crow laws that enforced segregation.

A key moment in my life's journey occurred when I was about nine years old. One day, during the devotional period at Short Journey School, an announcement was made that two kids would be chosen for scholarships to attend a Boy Scouts camp. My brother Curt and I had been Scouts so we were both in the running.

Our family members were traditional Baptists who went to church every Sunday. I wanted to go to camp really bad, so one Sunday I got down on my knees for the first time ever and prayed to God for the chance. I prayed really hard, so hard that tears flowed from my eyes. Sometime later an announcement was made at school that I and another boy, Clifford Vinson, had been selected to go to camp. I was so excited and felt really blessed to have this opportunity.

The camp was located in Rocky Mount, North Carolina. When the time came, I packed my things in a brand new chest, a hard green suitcase. This would be my first time away from home alone. Ma and Daddy drove me to the camp. It was about 45 miles away, which might not sound like a big distance. But it was a whole new world for me.

I was one of the few Black kids in camp, and it was my first exposure to being with a large group of White boys. But I had no qualms about it as I had a few friends who were White, especially Roger Stanley and Tommy Benton. They accepted me. Like me, Roger came from a struggling farm family and we would play baseball and basketball and race tractors against one another. His dad had John Deere tractors and my daddy had Farmalls and Massey Fergusons. I got the best of him most days. Tommy was the Cleveland High School principal's son and they had a nice basketball hoop in their back yard. I would go there and play with Tommy often and we became good friends.

At Scouts camp, all of the boys slept in rustic cabins. It was a cooperative living experience that reinforced the values of teamwork and respect for one another. Among the activities, we went on hikes and took part in events like tug of war, a competitive team experience in which we collectively tried to pull a rope against the other team to bring them over a white line. At night we sang songs and told jokes, sitting around a campfire.

But the biggest fire was the one that was lit in me. I was a different person when I left camp. I believed that opportunities would come – and even if the odds were stacked against me, I saw the possibility of a bigger, brighter future. Scouts camp gave me aspiration to put my hopes and dreams into action and I began to grasp that anything was possible with character and courage. The whole experience gave me faith that God could help make my dreams come true.

About the same time that I went to Boy Scouts camp, I began playing basketball. We built our own sandlot court out in front of the shed Daddy used for tractors and other equipment. My brother Jimmie would go out in the nearby woods to cut down trees and bring them back to use as posts. We nailed plank boards on them to serve as backboards and cut out the bottom of baskets to use as goals, until we eked out enough money to buy real rims. And we would make our own nets with tobacco twine.

Playing basketball was a joy. It was the best entertainment, better than watching TV, better than anything. Together with my brothers, cousins and friends, we would play hoops any time we could get a chance. If we got out of our farm chores for a half-hour lunch, we would eat quickly and spend the rest of the time playing on the makeshift court even when the temperature hit 100 degrees. If it had rained, we would take burlap bags used for cotton bales to sop up the puddles.

There was nothing better than playing basketball with and against friends like James Chester Williams and my cousin Moses Britt. We developed serious rivalries with the McClains and the Averys, who also had big families. My brother Jimmie would sent up games against them and other kids from Clayton, Selma and similar little towns in our part of North Carolina.

A few days following my retirement from Kent County, I received a letter from Kent Johnson, one of my playmates from the Johnson family on Powaton Road in nearby Wilson's Mills, where I was born. We had not been in contact with each other for decades. Kent reminded me of the playing conditions at their place. The makeshift dirt basketball court was located between the barn and drinking water well. The rim was scavenged from a junk pile and a tobacco pallet served as the backboard. As Kent reminded me, shots sometimes ricocheted off the rim and into the well, stopping play until we fished the ball out of the water. If the rebound went another way it could end up in the hog pen adjacent to the barn, which would force us to scrub the ball.

I played a lot against older guys in those days. It was the sort of thing that would either make one better or cause one to give up in frustration. There was no quit in me. At home I played against Curt, one-and-a-half years older and on his way to growing to be a 6'6" player. Jimmie was six years older than me, and he was a fanatic. I would compare him with Michael Jordan in his competitive fire, so it was a huge challenge to go up against him. When we were on the same side, he wouldn't accept anyone beating us. "You'd better check him, boy," he would demand of me even though I was usually playing against guys that had the advantage in size and age. To keep up, I began to develop an intensity about playing defense.

By the time I was 10 or 11, I dared to dream. I told my brothers and sisters that I was going to college to play basketball for the University of North Carolina, which was located in Chapel Hill. "No, you won't," said my older sister Jean, and she attempted to whup me. Later she would become positive and supportive of me. One day in school, my math teacher Mr. Sanders said, "Britt, what the heck are you doing?" The truth is, I was daydreaming about playing ball and going to college.

And then another amazing opportunity presented itself for my ninth grade year. I was bused to Cleveland High School, about 10 miles from my home. Cleveland High School had a solid basketball program, coached by Bruce Coats. He had played baseball at the University of North Carolina and and knew Dean Smith, who was on his way to becoming a legendary basketball coach at the school. Loyal to his alma mater, Mr. Coats painted his house in Carolina blue and white.

In the ninth grade, I became the first freshman to start on the Cleveland High School varsity basketball squad. I was also the first Black player on the team. Working on the farm helped me to grow into a stout and healthy kid, nearly 6'2", with broad shoulders, long arms and big feet that I got from my Dad. In fact, my size 15s were at least a couple sizes larger than my brothers who were all taller than me. When I was with the Los Angeles Lakers several years later, I found out that Kareem Abdul-Jabbar wore the same size shoe. Kareem kiddingly called me "Sasquatch," which is a creature that in folklore is also known as "Bigfoot."

I had friends and cousins who were good players, but I was so competitive that I was the one selected to play on the Cleveland High team. I was a strong rebounder and was not afraid to defend anyone. Success as a freshman had further fired up my dreams to play college ball in Chapel Hill.

However, by this time Daddy had faced the reality that farming was never going to provide the family much more than a subsistence living situation. His younger brother Paul had moved to Michigan and found work in a General Motors manufacturing plant, a union job that paid enough for a middle-class living. At my Uncle Paul's urging, Daddy moved up to Michigan, and he got hired for a job at a Buick foundry in Flint.

Daddy now wanted the rest of the family to join him. Mr. Coats offered me the chance to stay in North Carolina and live with him and his family. I was friends with his sons, Steve and Stan—we had hit it off, and I wanted to remain in Cleveland and on a path to play for Dean Smith. But Daddy said, "Hell no! You're coming with me." He wanted to keep all of the family together and move to where he now lived.

And so, after my freshman year of high school, I headed north with the rest of my family in 1969.

CHAPTER 3

State Championships

In Flint, I became a starting guard and forward on teams that won two basketball state championships. In my time there, I learned important lessons about how to be a team leader. But the move from North Carolina to Michigan did not go smoothly at first. I felt like a fish out of water when our family arrived in Flint, a blue-collar town located about 65 miles northwest of Detroit.

It took me a while to adjust to the northern, urban scene that was not as hospitable as the environment we had left behind in the south. The kids on our block and at school generally talked disrespectfully to each other, and newcomers became easy targets. They taunted us about the way we looked, the way we talked and the way we dressed. They made fun of our highwaters (also called flood pants) that came down only to our ankles. There was a lot of emphasis on talking cool and walking cool in order to fit in.

Fortunately, basketball helped break the barrier. Athletic competition is understood and respected across cultural lines, a factor that has opened doors for me many times during my life. Before long, my brothers Jimmie and Curt, my cousin Melvin Campbell and I were beating everyone on the basketball courts. We became known around town. That stopped most of the trash talking, and we made friendships based on knowing and respecting each other.

Flint's population was nearly 200,000 when we moved in. "Welcome to Buick City" read a large billboard on the edge of town, a nod to the local dominance of General Motors, then the largest automaker in the world. Flint was the birthplace of GM in 1908 and it was the site where the auto union movement began with a sit-down strike in the 1930s.

The city was home to Buick, Chevrolet and other GM factories that employed about 80,000 people when we arrived. Working-class people like Daddy who found jobs in those facilities could earn enough to provide a comfortable life for a family. Sadly, in the decades that followed, GM lost a big chunk of its business to global competitors. It also moved some of its work to foreign countries with cheaper labor. That resulted in many plant closings, erosion of the city's tax base, and devastating life changes for most of its citizens. The population now is about half what it was in Flint's heyday. And the city's financial stress led to a fateful decision to switch water sources, resulting in toxic levels of lead in drinking water that became a tragic national story.

My family lived in a three-bedroom house on Jamieson Street, only a few blocks from Flint Northern High School. I remember it was a very wholesome street. We became good friends with the Johnsons across the street and other families on the block. The city was very segregated along racial lines, and most African Americans lived in our section of town.

Along with some 2,000 other students, I attended Flint Northern. Being an athlete, my social life was pretty good and I made a lot of friends. I was one of the studious ones, a B student. Classmates saw me as a leader in the way I interacted with others and chose me to serve on the student council and then elected me class president my senior year. The late Sixties

As senior class president, I was part of Flint Northern High School's student council.

and early Seventies were turbulent years marked by struggles for racial equality and controversy over the Vietnam War. As senior class president, I needed to take on a leadership role by being the voice of reason during some tense situations.

The school had a rich tradition of athletics and also offered many extracurriculars. My younger brother Jay played bass in the school band and later toured with the professional gospel singing group, the Flint Cavaliers. My brother Curt was a basketball teammate and also played trombone in the marching band. Curt and I joined the school choir, where I sang tenor. Mr. Petry, the music department teacher, arranged for us to perform at events in the Flint area, and sometimes special guests would join us, like Jester Hairston, American composer, songwriter, actor, and choir conductor. Flint Northern also was involved in student exchange programs with schools in nearby cities like Midland and Bay City. My teammates and I felt like ambassadors representing our school.

I believe all of the activities helped keep us on the straight and narrow for the most part. A lot of our learning took place outside of the classroom, where we absorbed what it took to improve skills, work within a team concept, and compete on a high level. In addition, the adults who led these programs provided role models. One I remember in particular was assistant basketball coach Nate Perry, who operated with a great sense of discipline. He went on to become a district court judge in Genesee County, where Flint is located, and served on the bench for 30 years before retiring in 2020.

I am grateful for the chance to take part in extracurricular opportunities that helped me develop confidence and a sense of responsibility. But over the years, many of these programs have gone away because of budget concerns. This hurts every community in America, and disproportionately harms the students in poorer school districts. We need to figure out how to put those activities back in play.

I also landed my first paying job during my time at Flint Northern. For about three days a week after school, I would clean floors at Genesee County government offices. Oh, man, now I had $20 in my pocket and I didn't have to ask Ma or Daddy for money to see a movie or buy something. But I didn't work just for the cash. My job was to buff the floors of the Prosecutor's Office and Health Department, and I took pride in doing a good job. I held myself to a high standard, and have continued to do so throughout life. But as a high school student, I never thought that one day I would end up working in another county office, serving as administrator for Kent County in western Michigan.

In my sophomore year I began the basketball season on the junior varsity for the Flint Northern Vikings but soon moved up to varsity. Coach Dick Dennis put me in the starting lineup at guard, a position I would play through the rest of high school. He was a great guy and a good basketball coach who rarely showed his emotions, a demeanor similar to New England Patriots football coach Bill Belichick.

It was my first opportunity to play on a school team with my brother Curt, who was 6'6"tall and an excellent rebounder and defender. It was great to finally be on the same court with someone I had known all through my years growing up. We were close in age and growing up we worked on the farm together, wrestled with each other, and played backyard hoops. Because he was a year-and-a-half older than me, we never played on the same team in North Carolina. He attended Johnson County Training School in Smithfield, while I got bused to Cleveland High in Clayton in the first year of racially desegregating that school.

Our 1969-1970 season ended with a defeat in the regional finals of the state tournament. The loss propelled me to do whatever it took to get ready to do better in the next season. After my sophomore season, Coach Dennis left and was replaced by his assistant, Bill Frieder, who was also a math teacher at Flint Northern. He was a basketball junkie who went on to serve as head coach at the University of Michigan and Arizona State during a career that lasted more than three decades. He knew how to get talent to work together and was open to new ideas.

Frieder worked us very hard and he insisted that we play with physical toughness. But he also found ways to make it fun, using motivational schemes such as recognizing the player who got the most assists or most rebounds in a game with an ice cream dessert in the school cafeteria.

The Saginaw Valley Conference was considered one of the top high school basketball leagues in the country. In the 1970–71 season our big conference rival was Pontiac Central.

Ranked Number One in the state, they were led by Campy Russell, a tall and fluid player regarded in some circles as the best high school player in the country. Campy went on to earn All-American status at Michigan and became an NBA All-Star with the Cleveland Cavaliers.

Pontiac Central thumped us in the regular season, shooting 75% field goal percentage, and it appeared we might be headed for a rematch when our two squads made it to the semifinals of the Michigan high school tournament for Class A schools, the biggest in the state. We took care of business by beating Kalamazoo Central while most attention was given to the matchup between Russell's Pontiac Central and Detroit Kettering, which was led by Lindsay Hairston. Hairston, who would go on to play for Michigan State University (MSU) and then the NBA's Detroit Pistons, led Kettering to an upset win in the semifinals and that made them a solid favorite against us in the title game.

Frieder and assistant coach Perry devised a 2–3 zone defensive plan for us to stop Hairston, Kettering's 6'9" star. Whenever possible Curt, our center, would front Hairston and I would play behind him.

The Class A final was played at Crisler Arena on Michigan's campus. Our all-state forward Tom McGill—who would later end up at MSU with Hairston—scored 24 points but was hampered by foul trouble. We ended the third quarter with eight straight points for a 56–49 lead. Hairston scored 11 of his 21 points in the fourth quarter but we hung on to win, 79–78. I ended the game with 18 points and 29 boards, unheard of for a guy my size, but the defensive plan set me up in good position to get rebounds since I was playing between Hairston and the basket.

It was a great feeling to enjoy the accomplishment with my brother and my other teammates. The entire community celebrated, and it helped put Flint on a trajectory to becoming a hotbed of high school hoops. Basketball became a thread woven through the fabric of Flint. After us, the city produced top players such as Glen Rice, Eric Turner and Miles Bridges. Three city players that went on to MSU—Mateen Cleaves, Charlie Bell and Morris Peterson—became nationally known as The Flintstones when they led their team to the 2000 NCAA championship. But I like to think our 1971 team represented the beginning of the Flintstones.

During the summer after my junior year, I dated Kathy Henry, who lived down the street. She was my first girlfriend since the move to Michigan. Her family and ours were good friends and Kathy and I would sometimes go to movies with her mom and dad.

When Kathy became pregnant, I wanted to marry her. She said no, and she was adamant. She didn't have any interest in getting married or in going to college. Kathy said she wanted me to go on to college and that I would meet another girl. She was a little older than me, and she came from a family of Jehovah's Witnesses, but I don't know if those circumstances were any part of her thinking. It broke my heart that she didn't want to get married, but I had to accept this fact and find a way to move on and make it work the best for everyone.

It ended up with a wonderful outcome, but at the time it was very scary for me. Depressed, I really wanted to make it right. I had to accept the fact we weren't going to get married, had to move on and make it work as I eventually went on to school at the University of Michigan. Most people didn't know I had a son coming out of high school. My sisters and brothers wrapped their arms around my son, Eric, and he had a good life growing up with my family. I am very proud of how they surrounded and protected him as he grew up. They picked up the pieces for me. When I went to college, he couldn't stay on campus and could only just visit me. Having a child as a freshman at Michigan back then would have been a big detriment for a lot of people heading to college. I am grateful for what Kathy did in growing him up and the support that my family provided her. It helped me to stay true to my dream of attending college and playing on the basketball team.

There are a lot of stereotypes about African American men fathering children and then disengaging, but I stayed involved. I was never a stranger to my son. But school and basketball put requirements on my time, so it was my father, mother, sisters and cousins who had to become involved with Eric. You've heard the expression, "it takes a village," and in this case it was a family that surrounded him with love and protection. I'm very grateful for how they wrapped their arms around him and helped him to grow up.

I continued to stay tight with my son Eric throughout my time at University of Michigan. He would sometimes visit, and after I moved into an apartment my sophomore year he would spend the night or a weekend. My teammates knew him and accepted him as part of the mix. I didn't have money to pay child support while I was in school, but in later years I paid everything back to the Friend of the Court.

It was tough having a son at my age and not being around him all the time, but in the end there was a great result. As I write, Eric lives in Dallas, works for a large company that does logistics across the southern United States for major companies like Amazon and Staples. I'm thrilled that he has done really well and that the two of us have an amazingly good relationship today.

The Flint Northern Vikings faced major hurdles in our dream to repeat as state basketball champions. Leading scorer Tom McGill had graduated, along with other starters including my brother Curt, Ron Polk and Barry Menifee. There was no one left on our team taller than 6'4", which left us at a disadvantage against some teams with taller players.

Fortunately, three of us were able to sharpen our abilities during the summer by attending Dave Bing's basketball camp in Pocono Pines, a Pennsylvania town in the heart of the Pocono Mountains. At that time, Bing was playing for the NBA Detroit Pistons, building up his credentials to eventually enter the Basketball Hall of Fame.

Flint Northern teammates Terry Furlow and Dennis Johnson joined me in making the nearly 600-mile trip to the camp. Dave Simmons, an acquaintance of Frieder from Pontiac, Michigan, took an interest in helping talented young basketball players and drove us to camp that summer.

Simmons was a friend of the great Motown singer Marvin Gaye. Just a few months prior to our trip, Gaye had released his landmark album, "What's Going On," and we played that music all the way to the camp. Rolling Stone magazine now ranks this socially conscious record as the Number One album of all time, citing the way it helped change popular music by taking on issues like war, poverty, police brutality and environmental destruction. Simmons later moved to the Los Angeles area and stayed connected to Gaye and other Motown stars when the record label left Detroit for California. Tragically, Gaye was shot and killed by his father during an argument and Simmons was one of the first persons to reach the scene.

Bing and other NBA legends like Sam Jones and Wes Unseld were at the camp, giving us a unique opportunity to learn from the best. They showed us drills that they regularly did to master different aspects of the game and develop moves to improve our level of play. Love of the game was a bond that connected all of us, and the tough competition in the nightly contests raised our game. The experience helped us jell as a team, and we returned locked and loaded for the new season.

I was chosen to be captain of the team my senior season. During practice one day, Coach Frieder had us running sprints—we called them monster suicides. It was exhausting, and because a couple of players were goofing off, we had to go back and run them again. The fooling around continued after practice. At the water fountain near the locker room Furlow took a big swig of water and squirted it on me. That did it! I was furious and went after him. Lucky for both of us, Frieder broke it up.

Frieder took me aside and told me, "You can't do that." I didn't understand at first, as I thought as captain of the team I should be holding my teammate accountable for screwing around. Frieder responded with a list of reasons which came down to the necessity of the captain and leader of the team to show respect and tolerance for others. He urged me to overcome my discontent with certain players.

I trusted Frieder, and it was an important part of becoming a leader. I needed to overlook the faults of others and focus on the traits that could help the team. I had to refrain from complaining and whining about others because it would undermine group cohesion. The Bible tells us that God forced the Israelites to wander 40 years in the desert on the way to the Promised Land because they griped and doubted His word. Over the years, I have come to believe this is a lesson that American society needs to take to heart. Constant criticizing and blaming undercuts our efforts to move forward. We miss opportunities to solve problems because of all the negative energy.

Leveraging individual strengths set the Flint Northern basketball team on a path for success. I committed to become a facilitator on the squad and individual players eventually came to appreciate the value of putting team accomplishment first and foremost. Every one of our five starters—Terry Furlow, Dennis Johnson, Joel Ragland, Ricardo Jones and I—averaged in double figures and Raymond Bridges was key off the bench. On most teams, there is one superstar and the other guys fall in line. But in our case, our competitors couldn't just game plan to stop one guy. We liked to run and our opponents found they couldn't penetrate our tenacious defense because everyone was committed to it. And we relentlessly crashed the boards for rebounds.

We swept our conference season without losing a game, and then marched through the Class A state tournament to the finals. In front of a full house of 12,500 people at Michigan State's Jenison Field House, we again met our Saginaw Valley Conference rival Pontiac Central. Campy Russell had graduated, but Central still had his brother Larry who was a fine player that went on to play for Dick Vitale's University of Detroit teams. Larry eventually became a dentist and we still keep in touch.

It was a tough game, as expected. This is how the Michigan High School Athletic Association archives describes it:

Coach Bill Frieder's top-ranked Vikings, who had trailed by nine in the third quarter, delivered a knockout punch to their league rivals with six straight points in the final minute of the game. A basket by Northern's Terry Furlow with 54 seconds left tied the game at 69. Two free throws by Dennis Johnson and a bucket by sub Ray Bridges gave Northern a 73–69 lead

with 29 seconds to go to seal it. Wayman Britt led Northern
with 24 points with Furlow and Jones each contributing 15.

The 74–71 final score clinched a perfect 25–0 season. We had gone 47–2 over the course of two straight championship seasons, including a 33-game winning streak.

The Flint community celebrated again and we got the key to the city. Our State Representative Bobby Crim honored the team with a resolution in the legislature praising our feat. Dave Bing and Lem Barney, a Pro Football Hall of Fame defensive back for the Lions, were among those who attended our banquet that year.

As captain of the team, I received a number of accolades, including all-conference and all-state recognition. In later years, I was inducted into the Greater Flint Area Sports Hall of Fame and the Greater Flint African American Sports Hall of Fame. I appreciate every one of these awards, but I look at them as honors recognizing what we accomplished as a team.

Unfortunately, Flint Northern closed its doors in 2013, a victim of declining enrollment and school district financial troubles. Over the years, Northern won a total of 33 state championships in athletics.

Gone, but not forgotten. MLive, a media group that includes the Flint Journal, asked its readers in 2019 to vote on the Flint area's greatest high school sports team, and the 1972 Vikings basketball topped the list. And I will always have many good memories of my time at the school.

CHAPTER 4

Lessons In and Out of the Classroom

No one in my family had ever gone to college prior to my brother Curt who had graduated a year earlier from Flint Northern and was recruited to play basketball at Oakland University. Success on the basketball court, combined with a solid academic record, opened the door for me to be heavily recruited by several universities in the Midwest.

In the 1970s, high school coaches played a huge role in linking their players to colleges. They aren't as prominent in the recruiting game today with AAU showcases, clinics, camps and highlight videos providing other avenues of making connections. Flint Northern Coach Bill Frieder helped to put out the word about my abilities. I received letters from schools all over the Midwest, including a lot of the Big 10 universities plus others such as DePaul and Marquette. Coach Johnny Orr of Michigan and Coach Gus Ganakas of Michigan State recruited me heavily and I spent time visiting both schools to get a sense of their programs.

Michigan State made a good pitch but I eventually chose Michigan. The Spartans then pursued my Flint Northern teammate Terry Furlow who decided to join them and went on to lead the Big Ten in scoring his senior season. Furlow was an NBA first round pick with the Philadelphia 76ers and became a promising young player with the NBA's Utah Jazz, but tragically died in a car crash at age 25.

I chose Michigan and Coach Orr, in part because he was a very personable guy and I felt comfortable with him. He reminded me of Daddy, with his southern drawl and short cropped haircut. My mom also liked Orr the best. Her endorsement reinforced the way I was leaning, but in the end, it was my choice. Michigan was building a strong team, with high caliber players. The roster included prep All-American Campy Russell from Pontiac Central and Ernie Johnson from Grand Rapids Ottawa Hills. Henry Wilmore, an All-American guard from New York City, took me under his wing. John Lockard Jr. and Ken Brady were other highly regarded players and I hit it off right away with those guys.

Daddy drove me to Ann Arbor when it was time to start school in 1972 and I settled into the South Quad dorm on the U of M campus. A lot of basketball and football players lived there, and I made new friends among athletes and other students. Near the end of my freshman year, I moved into an apartment not far from the Law School with fellow teammate Bill Ayler, a very talented athlete from Detroit Northwestern. Bill and I became best friends and we did a lot together.

There were a lot of social issues and cultural changes going on all around us at that time. Students were caught up in these trends, and we couldn't help being affected. The military draft ended in 1973, so I didn't have to worry about that. But the Vietnam War was ongoing and wouldn't end until 1975, leading to campus demonstrations and questioning of authority by many students. Young people were testing new ways of living and relating. More women began seeking equal rights and opportunities.

The civil rights movement was also an important part of the changing scene. Michigan, like some other universities, created a department of Afro American and African Studies. Like others, I was struggling with how to grow up in America, be myself and be a part of a changing society. There was a concerted effort to shine a light on the Black experience and I learned a lot about my heritage by taking a class from Jon Lockard, one of the founding faculty members of the program. In addition to teaching, he was an artist who was co-founder and associate director of The Society for the Study of African Culture and Aesthetics and he served as a senior art advisor for the Dr. Martin Luther King Jr. memorial in Washington.

Professor Lockard's class strengthened the perception of myself and the value I brought to the table. Going to class and reading about different dynasties in Africa showed me that Black people had a remarkable history to cherish and a great deal to contribute today. We were blessed with talent and untapped potential. For me, it helped grow confidence that anything was possible.

As athletes, we were recruited to be members of fraternities. But several of us from Mr. Lockard's class decided we didn't want to go through the bother of hazing, so we created our own group called Black Inc. It better represented who we were as people. We didn't have a house like the fraternities with Greek letters did, but we socialized together and were all very supportive of each other.

Many of the colleges and universities in the southern states did not have any Black scholarship athletes on their teams until the late 1960s or early 1970s. Even in the rest of the country, there were unspoken quotas on how many African American players could be on a roster or on the basketball court as starters. Coaches were afraid of negative reactions by alumni and other boosters if they stepped over the real, though invisible, line regarding the number of Black players in the lineup.

At the time I attended Michigan, there were two African

American assistant basketball coaches, Jim Boyce and Richard (Bird) Carter, who may have helped reduce tensions. I owe a lot to Bird Carter who had also been on the team at Michigan a few years earlier and helped mentor me along the way. We also had winning seasons, and when you are an athlete on a successful team you get treated like a celebrity on campus. But bitterness over playing time issues boiled over at some other schools, including Michigan State where 10 Black basketball players walked out of a team meeting believing Coach Ganakas was not playing the best players because of a racial quota system. Ganakas suspended the players for one game, during which the Spartans suffered their worst loss in history, before reinstating them.

At the beginning of my freshman basketball season, it seemed clear that there were two factions on the team. The guys were just not playing together and it really hurt the squad's ability to realize its potential. I had been coming off the bench, but I went to Coach Orr and asked him to give me a chance to start at guard. He did, putting me in the opening lineup at Michigan's Crisler Arena against our in-state rival MSU. Prior to the 1972–1973 season the NCAA had barred freshmen from playing college varsity basketball, so it turned out I became the first one to ever start in Michigan's program.

During the game, I got the crowd excited early by throwing a pass behind my back. Orr didn't care for that. "Britt, cut that fancy crap out," he told me. I did and focused on being unselfish and facilitating other players to do their best. We won that game.

I approached each contest with the attitude that I acquired playing with my brothers back in North Carolina, which is that we had to work together. It wasn't about how many points I scored. It was about getting the ball to who was open and getting it in the basket. No one is more important than the team and it was about winning games.

We finished in the middle of the Big Ten pack that season, and some key seniors departed including Henry Wilmore, Ernie Johnson, John Lockard and Ken Brady. We weren't expected to be as good my sophomore year.

Just before practices for the 1973–74 season began, I got sick with strep throat. I spent time in the infirmary and couldn't practice for more than a week. Coach Orr had penciled me in at guard for my sophomore season, but freshman Steve Grote was looking good in practice and Orr wanted to pair him with Joe Johnson as the starting guards. When I returned to practice, Orr said he wanted me to play forward.

I was just under 6'2" tall and I never imagined I would play forward against players several inches taller than me in the physical Big Ten conference. Michigan had some tradition of playing smaller guys at forward, like Henry Wilmore and Richard Carter before me. Orr put talent where he thought it would best help the team, and he believed my athletic ability and tenaciousness would be an asset.

The competition for starting forward came down to me and Bill Ayler, my roommate and best friend. We battled hard, and even got into a fight one time during practice. I learned to welcome the challenge of defending taller opponents and won the starting assignment, although I hated the fact that it had to be at the detriment of Bill, my best friend and roommate at that time.

Orr was like a father figure to me, and I trusted him. Playing for him, I realized the importance of team culture to any organization, including athletics, business and government. Culture comes from a mindset that establishes core values, expectations and the way people relate to each other. As Lou Gerstner learned during his days as CEO at IBM, "Culture is not part of the game, it is the game."

Orr was an empowering type of coach. He knew X's and O's, put structure in place, and occasionally he would get on a player. But he gave players a lot of freedom during the game. It was our job to win. His style encouraged us to be engaged and accountable in solving problems on the court.

Our team played a very up-tempo game that emphasized sharing the ball. We set a Wolverines single-game record with 32 assists in a contest against Purdue, a mark that stood for 13 years. Unranked to begin the season, we went 8–2 in the nonconference schedule and then opened the Big Ten schedule by knocking off defending conference champion Indiana in a game at Crisler Arena. Later in the season, the Hoosiers returned the favor by beating us on their home court. That left us tied atop the conference standings and set up a neutral site contest in Champaign, Illinois to determine which team would go to the NCAA tournament, which consisted of only 24 teams in those days. There, we beat Bobby Knight's squad to put Michigan in the national tourney for the first time since 1966.

We were slotted into the Mideast Regional in Tuscaloosa, Alabama, and after a bye we went up against Notre Dame in the Sweet Sixteen. The Fighting Irish were 24–2 and riding high after beating UCLA a couple of months earlier, snapping the Bruins' record 88-game winning streak, a record that might never be surpassed. I was going to be guarding Adrian Dantley, a 6'5" freshman forward from Washington, D.C. who was averaging 18 points a game.

The day before the game, I visited the University of Alabama campus in Tuscaloosa with teammates Campy Russell and Joe Johnson. There we met up with Notre Dame players Gary Brokaw and John Shumate, and they started talking smack. They boasted about how I wouldn't be able to handle Dantley.

Preparation is essential to being able to achieve goals when the pressure is on. In those days we didn't have a lot of videos to watch other players, so we relied on news clipping and scouting reports on tendencies. The report on Dantley was that he liked to go to his left. My plan was to get on his right side but anticipate his going left. I also had a strategy to run him up and down the court as fast as I could and tire him out guarding me.

We won the game, 77–68, and Dantley scored only two points. Afterward, Sports Illustrated quoted him as saying his legs "felt like log cabins." Years later, I heard that he told someone, "Wayman Britt is the reason I realized I needed to lose weight." That worked out pretty well for him as a slimmer Dantley ended up twice leading the NBA in scoring on his way to being elected to the Basketball Hall of Fame.

With a trip to the Final Four on the line, we were then edged out by Al McGuire's Marquette team, 72–70. McGuire was a wizard as coach and his team was led by future NBA All-Star Maurice Lucas. Marquette went to the NCAA finals where they lost to champion North Carolina State. Our season was over. But we had established a good foundation for the program to continue as a strong national contender.

All my experiences during this time contributed to the man I became. This included the summers, when I earned some money taking blue-collar jobs. I was hired at a General Motors truck plant in Flint for two years, working on an assembly line and later in the security area. I took a job with Allied Van Lines in Ann Arbor another summer, loading and unloading trucks.

These summer jobs made me realize how difficult the work world is for many people. On a moving auto assembly line, picking up fenders and attaching them was a tough job. I walked out of there with an appreciation for the professionalism and the capability these workers needed to have. These are honorable people doing honorable jobs.

I also went to gyms to play basketball when I could, sometimes going to the court at Eastern Michigan University in Ypsilanti, not far from the U of M campus. Another guy who played there sometimes was George Gervin, who was beginning to blossom in his professional career in the ABA and who eventually became an all-time great in the NBA. The ball really moved around the court in those games. I loved playing with him. Gervin earned the nickname, "The Iceman," for his cool demeanor while performing creative new moves on the court during a career that landed him in the Basketball Hall of Fame.

Gervin gave me a pair of shoes from an up-and-coming company called Nike. Unfortunately, Nike had not yet perfected its products, and the shoes split on the sides when I wore them in a Michigan game against a Tennessee team which included Ernie Grunfeld and Bernard King. I had to borrow a pair of shoes from a backup player, Tom Staton. The problem was that I wore size 15 and Staton's shoes were size 13. We lost the game by one point, 82–81. "Damn it, Britter," said Orr. "Where the hell did you get those shoes?"

A different summer experience involved our team after my junior year, a season in which we finished second to Indiana in the Big Ten and then lost in the opening round of the NCAA tourney to eventual champion UCLA. In August, the team left for Egypt for a 15-day goodwill tour. We played the Egyptian national team seven times and won all the games. The contests helped us sharpen our play, but perhaps more importantly, the overall experience strengthened our bonds.

We visited the Egyptian Museum and the Citadel in Cairo, saw pyramids and the Great Sphinx, and swam in the Mediterranean. We were the talk of the town in Cairo and Alexandria, and the Egyptian people were very good to us. However, we were shocked by the poor conditions that most Egyptians lived in. Many of the people lived in small apartments where some raised chickens that they killed for their meals. Most of our games were played on dirt courts. The hotel that we stayed in was infested with large roaches in the rooms, and all the lights would go off at night except in the hallways. I remember hearing bombs going off, as tensions rose between Egypt and Israel.

When the team returned home, we really appreciated America and many of the things we take for granted. Playing in difficult conditions brought us closer together as a team. The shared experience helped to mold us and to take our game to the next level.

I served as captain my senior year and I knew it was important that I set a positive tone for us to win. It was the same as when I was at Flint Northern. When you're the captain, it isn't about how many points you score. It's about the example and the sacrifices you make, and I tried to maintain an attitude of confidence. Just as it is in business and government, the culture of a team must be right. Our culture was built around toughness, self-sacrifice, and playing team ball.

Coach Orr and others called me "Britter." I took it as recognition that I was always positive and committed to outworking most people. Sometimes other players would ask me to stop making them look bad in the wind sprints and going hard after rebounds during practice. My attitude was based on what I learned from Daddy back in North Carolina when I was getting up at 3 or 4 a.m. to do farm work—don't make excuses, get the job done. Sometimes, Orr also referred to me as "Coach." In later years, he called me twice to see if I was interested in joining his coaching staff, but I turned him down as I was focused on a career in business management.

Playing forward, I was still going up against taller opponents. I was very observant and anticipated what those guys liked to do. And I needed to play with heart, determination and a belief in myself. I used my body, leverage, forearm, whatever I had to do. They didn't like it. I wasn't a dirty player —it was more of a chess game for me. I found ways to put on a little pressure to make them uncomfortable.

From that experience, I did gain recognition as a stopper and I hope a lot of the young men that have come along after me benefited from that example. I accepted what the program wanted me to do. Good teams become better when members sacrifice themselves, putting themselves on the line for each other. As captain, I learned that sometimes it is better to lead from behind. There are times you have to pull back in favor of the hot hand, the player who has the right formula on a particular day.

The starters for our 1975-76 team were Rickey Green, Phil Hubbard, John Robinson, Steve Grote and me. Just like the Flint Northern state champions four years earlier, every starter averaged double figures in points. You couldn't beat us by stopping just one player.

Indiana was the clear favorite in the Big Ten and they swept through their schedule undefeated. We finished second at 14-4 and gave the Hoosiers their biggest scare. After losing to them by six points at home in January, I was concerned that Coach Orr was not playing the best lineup because of racial issues. My old Flint Northern coach, Bill Frieder, was now an assistant at Michigan and I went to his house to make my case that Dave Baxter should replace Steve Grote as a starting guard. Baxter was lighting it up in practice. He was a sharpshooter and his presence would open the floor for our inside players. Grote eventually proved himself a worthy player and the Wolverines now have a Steve Grote Hustle Award that is presented each year. But at the time I lobbied for Baxter, Grote was not playing well.

However, making that change would have meant all five starters would be African American. Frieder said he wouldn't talk to Coach Orr about the issue. I'm sure he was concerned about eventually moving up and did not want to cross that line. He told me I had to talk to coach, so soon afterward I went into Orr's office to urge him to start Baxter.

"Britter, what are we going to do about the alumni?", Orr asked. "What are we going to do about the boosters?" I said, "Coach, I don't know, but you've got to put the best players on the floor." We didn't walk off the floor in protest like the Michigan State players did a few years earlier, but I have always wondered how the season would have turned out if Baxter had gone into the starting lineup.

In the early 1990s, Michigan Coach Steve Fisher faced the heat and started a group of immensely talented Black freshmen who became known as the Fab Five. I didn't realize how fanatical some alumni were against them until years later, when an ESPN documentary revealed the racist hate mail and threats that were directed at them and their coach. But they were winners, and most Michigan fans embraced them. Their play and their style made them virtual rock stars across the country, and they generated huge merchandising sales for the university.

A month after losing to Indiana at home in January 1976, we went to Bloomington to play them again. We had them on the ropes in this one. Indiana's All-American forward Kent Benson scored on a tip-in at the end of regulation and we ended up losing a heartbreaker in overtime.

But for the third straight year we were selected for the

NCAA tournament, which now had 32 teams. Our first game against Wichita State in Denton, Texas, was almost our last. But Rickey Green scored on a baseline jumper with six seconds left to pull it out, 74–73.

The regionals in Louisville were next, starting against Notre Dame. Adrian Dantley was now a junior, had averaged nearly 29 points a game and was a consensus All-American.

The Michigan team cut down the net when we beat Missouri to advance to the NCAA Final Four, and as captain it was my honor to finish the job.

But he was pretty much a one-man team, and we managed an 80–76 win over the Irish. Next up in the regional final was Big Eight champion Missouri, led by Willie Smith, a high-scoring guard who went by the nickname "Mister Magic." He put on a show, but we were a team and a 95-88 win sent us to the Final Four in Philadelphia.

Two unbeaten teams were still alive. Rutgers, at 31-0, was one of them and we faced them in the semifinals. My primary defensive assignment was to hound their leading scorer, 6'5" forward Phil Sellers. We played an excellent all-around game, holding Sellers to only 12 points and Rutgers to 39 percent shooting. The 86–70 victory meant we were going to the Finals. In the other semifinal, unbeaten Indiana smacked UCLA 65–51.

The Indiana versus Michigan game marked the first time two teams from the same conference played in the NCAA championship game. We had lost twice to them in the conference season in games that were decided by only a play or two. The importance of preparation really got my attention against Indiana as they were the most prepared team we ever played. Unlike some of the other teams we played earlier in the tournament, they were not overly reliant on one star. Scott May, Quinn Buckner, Kent Benson, Tom Abernathy and Bobby Wilkerson were all major contributors in one way or another.

We got off to a good start and led 35–29 at halftime, but the Hoosiers came back strong in the second half to take the lead. When we committed a lot of desperation fouls late in the game, they hit their free throws and pulled away to win, 86-68. Indiana finished 32–0. That 1975–76 Indiana squad remains the last college basketball team to finish the season undefeated.

I look back at that game and realize what a unique opportunity it presented. I took from it the need to prepare yourself, believe in yourself and really work hard because you might never get a chance like that again. One day your number is going to be called and you don't want to look back and realize you were unprepared. We achieved a lot, but when I think back, I wonder if we could have done a little more preparation to win it all.

At the end of the season, I became the first Michigan player to receive the Defensive Player of the Year Award and I am honored that the team now gives a Wayman Britt Outstanding Defensive Player Award every season. At the end of my four-year career, the athletic department and basketball office recognized me with the "I've Been Hit by Britt Club" commendation, which consisted of a list of 18 opposing top-name players across the country that I had the distinction of shutting down., including UCLA's Keith Wilkes, Indiana's Scott May, Wisconsin's Kim Hughes, South Carolina's Nate Davis, Notre Dame's Adrian Dantley and Michigan State's Terry Furlow.

Even though I was a good athlete, I wanted to be more than that. As a student, I changed majors and dropped some courses over time. I didn't graduate in four years but I returned to school later to get my bachelor's degree in sports management and communications. I was aiming for a career in radio and TV broadcasting, but it didn't work out.

I benefited greatly from my time at the University of Michigan, learning lessons that I have carried with me for life. The experience reinforced the idea that I needed to embrace and accept the differences between me and other players. I emphasized doing things right, but they had certain attributes that I didn't have and I came to realize there must be a balance of different styles. It is important to have a bit of swagger and bravado, something that great players like Magic Johnson and Michael Jordan had. At Michigan, I overcame my discontent with some players. I learned to love those guys and we had some special days together.

The most important thing is the team. Success depends on more than one or two people. You can't have different people pulling different ways. It's the bench, the ball boy, the water people, the cheerleaders—they all have a part. It's the entire team. And the lesson that everyone has a part to play carries over into any kind of organization.

CHAPTER 5

A New Path

At basketball practice one day at the University of Michigan's Crisler Arena, the football team was also working out in the building. We had some fun racing each other that day, and I went up against Gil Chapman, a running back and kick returner for the Wolverines gridiron squad. I beat him in a dash, and it seems that word got around. Michigan football coach Bo Schembechler would come to a lot of our games at Crisler and asked me two different times to come out for his team. I turned him down, as I had never played football in high school or college and I preferred to focus on basketball. But he thought my quickness, speed and agility gave me the skill set to succeed as a defensive back.

After my senior year the Los Angeles Lakers chose me in the fourth round of the NBA draft, but pro football teams also showed interest. Legendary Green Bay Packers quarterback Bart Starr called me, and the Detroit Lions invited me to attend a skills camp. Bobby Mitchell, a Hall of Fame wide receiver who was now working in the Washington Redskins front office, also contacted me. And it was the Redskins who selected me in the 13th round of the National Football League draft.

George Allen was the head coach, Calvin Hill (the father of Grant Hill) had just signed a free agent contract to join the team as a running back, and Billy Kilmer was the starting quarterback. It seemed apparent that a young Joe Theismann was on his way to winning the starting QB role. Coming out of high school in New Jersey, Theismann had been recruited to play basketball by the University of North Carolina—ironically, I had grown up hoping to play for the Tar Heels. As a prep player, he was not considered a top football prospect because he played for a team that basically ran the football. But Notre Dame football coach Ara Parseghian noticed his good basketball footwork and took a chance on him. During tryout camp, I found out Theismann still had some great basketball moves when he beat me in a half-court game.

I didn't end up playing pro football but a pivotal moment in my life occurred during the camp as a result of rooming with Denny Duron, a quarterback from Louisiana Tech who had led that team to back-to-back national championships in Division II. He was the son of a preacher from the Shreveport, Louisiana area. Although I had been raised in the Baptist Church as a boy in North Carolina, I had not gone to church faithfully for some time. Duron gave me an annotated Bible and we held discussions that completely changed my life in terms of what I was going to be about.

When I embraced the Lord, it motivated me to become a better person in terms of discipline and temperance. I came to understand that God loves me, and this knowledge strengthened my belief that good things can happen. When I would encounter difficult times, I had faith that something better was ahead. The doubt about my potential to succeed in life diminished when I had the right relationship with God. I believed there was a purpose for my life and that there was a higher power moving me toward my intended destiny.

I was on a different path when I left camp and my faith

provided a compass for a lot of big decisions that I made in life. It is a big reason that I eventually came to realize my purpose in life was to serve others.

One day in practice at the Washington Redskins tryout camp I realized how fast the wide receivers really were. That was a factor that ultimately led to my decision to leave camp to stay with basketball and sign a contract with The Lakers. I looked forward to playing in the NBA with a team coached by Jerry West and with talented players like Kareem Abdul-Jabbar and Lucius Allen.

In those days, I tried to emulate one basketball player in particular—Julius Erving, best known as "Dr. J." I encountered him briefly at the 1976 NCAA Finals in the hallway at the Spectrum in Philadelphia. He was wearing a brown leather suit, and I was on my way to the locker room. "What's up, Wayman?", he said, and I replied, "What's up, Doc?" That was so cool!

On the court, Dr. J was bringing a new artistry to the game with the way he could hang in the air and deliver breathtaking dunks and other shots. But it wasn't just his on-court moves that inspired me. I admired his professionalism. He epitomized excellence in character, and his marriage to the elegant woman Turquoise influenced my decision to get more settled and try to build a life with a partner. Just out of college, I married Marilyn Skinner, who I had met at Michigan in the South Quad. I tried to make it work, but looking back, I think I wasn't clear on what was best for me. Like Dr. J and Turquoise, Marilyn and I ended up having four children. And like Dr. J and Turquoise, our marriage ended in divorce.

After my brief fling with the NFL, Marilyn and I piled all

of our stuff in my 1970 Mercury Cougar and U-Haul trailer and drove cross-country to Los Angeles. The Lakers put me back at the guard position, even though I had played forward the previous three seasons at Michigan. At 6 feet, 1 inches, my natural position was in the backcourt but Coach Johnny Orr had moved me to forward because he felt my athletic ability at that position would best help the team. Now I had to learn all over again how to play guard. Going in, my left hand play was not as strong as it would have been had I remained at guard my whole career.

These days, NBA contracts are much more lucrative and university athletes can easily transfer schools, so many players make their college decision on how the choice will help them succeed in the professional game. But during my time it was about the team and what made sense in the coach's eyes. Perhaps I would have had more NBA success if I had been kept at the guard position. But looking back at what I have accomplished, I believe the path I ended up taking helped me grow more as a person and a leader, and led to a more fulfilling life.

I was playing well in the Lakers preseason, and felt I had a good relationship with Kareem, who kidded me about my size 15 shoes by referring to me as "Sasquatch." I felt they appreciated that I was a fierce competitor. One day at practice, I was wrestling for a rebound with power forward Kermit Washington. I guess he didn't appreciate the way I was being physical and he came after me to fight. Luckily, others broke it up before he could unleash a swing. Washington had huge arms and had taken boxing lessons. A year later, Washington threw a punch that fractured the face of Houston Rockets forward Rudy Tomjanovich and left him unconscious, an incident that changed the trajectory of both men's lives.

I stayed with the Lakers until the last game of the exhibition season, when the team made the decision to release me.

One circumstance that worked against me was that the American Basketball Association had forced a merger with the NBA that year. Four teams were absorbed into the NBA while other ABA teams folded, expanding the number of players coming into the league. The Lakers had picked Don Chaney and Mack Calvin from the ABA and had signed free agent Cazzie Russell —and all of them were on no-cut contracts.

I went to see General Manager Bill Sharman after I was cut. I told him the decision was a real blow, but he said they had to move on. I stayed in California for two weeks, hoping something would happen to turn things around, but then headed back to Michigan.

The Detroit Pistons then picked up my rights. But their roster was full, meaning I would have to sit out the balance of the season and then come to training camp the following year. Marilyn and I headed to Grand Rapids to assist her mother, who had gotten ill. I took a job with Michigan National Bank-Central, starting as a cashier and later moving to assistant branch manager and then loan collections officer.

I got in great shape by working out at 21st Century Health Spa, and became stronger by using weights. And I regularly made the two-hour drive to Detroit to play basketball at Ceciliaville, a place that came to be known as "The Saint." It was a west side gym for a Catholic parish high school that closed in the late 1960s. The gym was then opened up to the neighborhood, with leagues forming for all ages and levels of players. And then one year Dave Bing of the Pistons used Ceciliaville to work out while he held out in a contract dispute. Word got around that this was the place to test and prove your game. Over the years The Saint drew top talent, including Magic Johnson, George Gervin, Earl Cureton, Jalen Rose and Chris Webber.

When I showed up for the Pistons preseason camp in 1977,

I didn't realize there were three distinct cliques on the team. There were the veterans like Bob Lanier and Willie Norwood, the players from the East Coast such as Chris Ford and Kevin Porter, and younger guys like Marvin Barnes and Eric Money whom I felt most comfortable with. Had I known the situation, I might have tried harder to develop a relationship with Lanier, who was the franchise's highest paid player. We played an intra-squad game at my old home court, Crisler Arena in Ann Arbor, where I was the leading scorer and fans who remembered my college career cheered me on. Lanier mockingly commented and scoffed at the positive reception I received.

I made the team, beating out all of the other rookies and free agents vying for the same position as me. Then the bottom fell out again. The league was having financial issues, and during the summer the owners had tried to reduce team rosters from 12 players to 11 in order to save money. A legal challenge by the Players Association delayed the implementation, but after the season began the owners won the case.

The Pistons needed to cut one player from the roster, and the choice came down to me or Pistons veteran Willie Norwood, who was a 6'8" forward and was part of the older veterans' faction. Lanier at 6'11" was conveniently out sick and Marvin Barnes at 6'8" was out hurt when the decision had to be made, and the Pistons figured they needed the frontcourt size of Norwood and rookie Ben Poquette at 6'9". I was the odd man out.

The Pistons wanted me to go play for a team in the Eastern League where Jack McCloskey had been a general manager and Herb Brown a coach. Later, both men ended up in the same position with the Detroit Pistons. The idea was that Detroit would recall me if an opening developed because of injury or some other reason. But I turned them down, as our daughter Raven had just been born and I was offered a spot as one of five management trainees at Steelcase, a major office furniture manufacturer based in Grand Rapids.

The next year, the Pistons invited me back. But they wanted me to come to the free agent/rookie camp instead of the regular preseason workouts, as I had done in the previous season. This was a step back for me. I wrote a letter to the team's new coach, Dick Vitale. I pointed out that I had made the team the previous year and that I had led the Ceciliaville league in scoring during that summer. I felt I was a bona fide NBA player and I didn't believe I should have to risk my new career at Steelcase for the chancy proposition of making the Pistons roster from rookie camp.

But Vitale was adamant in his position that I had to come to the rookie camp. It was a very difficult decision, and I chose not to go to the Pistons and instead stayed on the path that had opened to me at Steelcase.

For years afterward, I would have dreams of competing in the NBA, hovering over the top of the rim and scoring at a prolific pace. My decision haunted me for a long time and I was filled with doubts over whether I had chosen wisely.

But as life went on, I realized I had made the right move.

CHAPTER 6

What Will You Tell Them?

"To whom much is given, much will be required" is a Biblical verse that informs those who have been blessed with talent, knowledge and wealth that they are expected to use these blessings to benefit others. There is a painting that hangs in my home office as a reminder of this responsibility. I found it one day during a visit to the Bayard Gallery of Fine African American Art and Books in Grand Rapids, owned by George Bayard. It is a portrait of the faces of several Black boys, each one looking straight at the viewer. The artist was the late Jon Lockard, my professor in Afro American and African Studies at the University of Michigan. The painting carries the title, "What Are You Going to Tell Them?"

Knowing Lockard, I could imagine him saying: "For those of you who have been given the opportunity to go to the University of Michigan and have been given the platform that you have, what are you going to do with it and what are you going to tell the people who came after you?" When I didn't finish my degree in four years, it was Lockard who called me to task. "What are you doing? What are you waiting for?", he asked. He was telling me that I needed to wake up and use my potential to make a difference in the lives of other African Americans who had not had my opportunities. And so, I went back and finished my studies for a degree in communications and sports management.

"What Are You Going to Tell Them?" is a provocative question and deserves an answer that encompasses our experiences, our goals and our commitment to creating a roadmap for younger generations to follow. For America to evolve to a more equitable society, we need to figure out how we can all live and prosper together. We are all fundamentally the same as human beings. And as a country, we are no better than our weakest link.

I grew up in Smithfield Township, North Carolina, just 10 miles outside of the city of Smithfield where the billboard from a hate group that used terror and intimidation to protect white supremacy greeted you as you came to town. As you

Ku Klux Klan billboards like this one greeted visitors to Smithfield, North Carolina, a short distance from where I grew up in North Carolina.

crossed the Neuse River on U.S. 70, you saw the message that featured a cloaked-in-white figure carrying a burning cross while riding a horse. "Join and Support The United Klans of America Inc.", the billboard advocated. "Help Fight Communism and Integration!" A separate strip at the bottom read "Welcome to Smithfield."

I once shared my recollection about the billboard with Herman Boone when he visited in Grand Rapids. The celebrated football coach, portrayed by Denzel Washington in the movie "Remember the Titans," recollected the sign because his all-Black E.J. Hayes High School team would sometimes make the trip from Williamston to Smithfield to play the Johnston County Training School.

Even though Boone's teams at Hayes won 99 games and lost only eight times, the school board demoted him to assistant coach when the school became racially integrated in 1969. Boone resigned and two years later became the head coach at T.C. Williams High School in Alexandria, Virginia, a city torn apart by racial tensions. The first task for Boone and his diverse coaching staff was to get players to resolve their suspicions and direct their energy to the common goal of winning. This team of Black and White teenage boys learned mutual respect and went on to win a state championship.

Boone understood how people tend to carry negative assumptions toward those who look different than them. If you don't deal with individuals up close and get to know their talents, capabilities and assets, you won't trust them to contribute to the success of a team or organization. This distrust prevents individuals and groups from reaching their full capability.

I have encountered overt racism in my life, and it takes a tremendous toll. "What are you doing here?" is a question I was boldly asked once when I became part of an organization and the only African American in the room. The question was posed by a person of wealth and prominence whom I'd never before met. I surmised the reason that this happened is because that person not only thought that way, but probably felt safe enough to say it and understood that others in the room had the same view.

This kind of racism is slightly less blatant than that Ku Klux Klan billboard outside my hometown. America has made advancement in race relations—often slow, sometimes painful—since then. The fact that I was chosen in 2018 as the first African American to hold the job of administrator for Kent County is evidence of advancement. That wouldn't have been within the realm of possibility for a Black man when I was growing up. Nor could we have imagined that a Black person, like Barack Obama, could be elected president.

Despite this tangible headway, most Americans still believe racial and ethnic discrimination remains a big problem in the country, according to several surveys. Meaningful change is needed to resolve the problems of individual racism and systemic discrimination.

When I first saw the video on the death of George Floyd, I couldn't watch it all the way through. It took me back to a day when I was in high school in Flint. I was walking at about dusk when a police car rolled up and officers asked me to put my hands on their car so they could frisk me, because someone had committed a robbery in the community. The fear that gripped me then was the same fear that filled me when I saw the scene of George Floyd gasping for breath as a White police officer kneeled on his neck for more than nine minutes on a Minneapolis street.

Floyd's death generated protests around the country as well as in some foreign countries. In Kent County, I saw that many residents were truly concerned about what was happening and wanted to work together to ensure every human being is treated as an equal member of society, getting fair treatment all through the criminal justice system. We were all hurting and attempting to deal with the aftermath of something we knew should never have happened.

I believe strongly in the power of listening if we are going to change the world. Listening builds trust and loyalty, helps to head off problems and provides important perspective from different viewpoints. In Kent County, I sought to open channels connecting the Board of Commissioners, employees in all departments, businesspeople, community groups and individual citizens. Allowing more voices to be heard is crucial to understanding what needs to happen to improve the way we live and work together.

Reaching the goal of a more just society is not an individual race, it is more like a 400-meter relay. We are dependent on one another. On the county level, it means making sure that our leg of the race in administration and the Board of Commissioners is run at the most equitable and just way possible. Then, when the baton is passed on to the sheriff's office, circuit court, district court, prosecutor's office, veterans services, public works, drain commissioner, clerk's office and health department, they can run their legs of the race in a way that ensures we all win.

George Floyd's death raised awareness of the way some police officers commit unnecessary and heinous violence against African Americans. To be clear, not every officer behaves that way. Upstanding officers protect the community and their moral standards set an important example for the rest of us.

As Kent County Sheriff Michelle LaJoye-Young recognized, it is critical for law enforcement to treat everyone with respect and dignity. The sheriff helped establish more ways for officers to get involved with the community, focused on improving diversity in hiring and promoting, and banned practices such as choke holds. In the wake of protests that sometimes turned destructive, she acknowledged there is a delicate balance between protecting free speech while also defending the rights of property owners. Officer training seeks to give sheriff deputies the tools to lower the temperature and de-escalate violence. These are examples of seeds that will hopefully grow into meaningful change.

The George Floyd tragedy also led many of us to reflect on what we have witnessed during our lifetimes. Martin Luther King Jr. once said, "The arc of the moral universe is long, but it bends toward justice." But the arc doesn't bend by itself. It takes effort by a host of courageous people to bend the arc. It requires transformative leaders and others who are willing to sacrifice in order to make it happen. There are historical moments when the right person comes along, when those who thirst for justice are eager for transformation, and when people are willing to reach across the aisle long enough to make a difference.

Change is difficult for most people, as they are uncomfortable with the uncertainty that comes with breaking long-standing habits. Until MLK came on the scene, nothing had been done for many years to advance civil rights. MLK was the lighting rod that forced people to see the inequities endured by African Americans. He led a movement that led to passage of the federal Civil Rights Act and Voting Rights Act. I believe this movement also led to heightened recognition of civil liberties for others who incurred discrimination, such as women and gays.

We all experience change on a personal level. One major change that directly affected my life occurred several years after the Supreme Court ruled that racial segregation of public-school students was unconstitutional. It was the beginning of the end for Jim Crow laws that claimed to provide "separate-but-equal" services based on race, but which were in fact not at all equal. Desegregation resulted in my being bused to Cleveland High School, where I became the first freshman and first Black player to start on the varsity basketball team.

One night, our Cleveland Rams basketball squad played a team from an all-Black school. When a fight broke out, our players were ushered to a safe spot in the balcony. One of my teammates looked at me and asked, "Which team are you with?" I replied, "What are you talking about? I'm on my team, the Cleveland Rams!" That was the only time where the race issue ever got brought up on that team. It shone a light on underlying distrust, but in the long run we learned to work together. These were good guys, and I am still in touch with some of them.

I have experienced how sports help break down some of the racial barriers. Growing up, I became friends with two White boys, Roger Stanley and Tommy Benton. We played basketball and baseball together, which helped me more easily adapt when I was bused to Cleveland High School. But I still witnessed vestiges of White guys being favored on teams that I played on, even if they didn't have the skill sets that earned them the time. And it's obvious that even when African Americans dominate the playing field they remain vastly underrepresented in the coaching and ownership ranks.

African Americans often come up against the prejudice that their lack of representation in lack of leadership positions means they can't lead and it reinforces the narrative that this country is not ours too. Systemic racism bolsters this message by stacking the odds, making it more difficult to succeed in the economy and society. Among the persistent racial inequities is the poverty rate, substandard schools, unemployment, the net worth of Black families, incarceration rates and a wealth gap aggravated by a legacy of redlining that made it difficult for Blacks to get loans for home ownership.

African Americans rarely see themselves represented in history classes. This lack of depiction does tremendous damage to Black people who are reminded day in and day out that they aren't as valued as a person with light skin. Over time, this message keeps repeating itself, and the self-doubt and the fear grows. These negative experiences undermine a person's ability to reach their potential. In his book, *Mis-Education of the Negro*, Carter G. Woodson affirmed, "When you control a man's thinking, you do not have to worry about his actions. You do not have to tell him not to stand here or to go yonder. He will find his 'proper place' and will stay in it. You do not need to send him to the back door. He will go without being told. In fact, if there is no back door, he will cut one for his special benefit."

Very few are blessed with the chance I had in Jon Lockard's course to learn the value of Black history, that our ancestors were kings and queens in Africa and that we have amazing capacity to contribute. The class helped to assure me that I was a person of significance—and therefore, anything was possible. I wish every young Black person could learn about themselves from such a course so they could appreciate their heritage.

A shortage of role models also hinders the ability of young Blacks to imagine a positive outcome for their future. Campy Russell, my friend and former Michigan basketball teammate, reminded me of this when I was considering the top job of administrator for Kent County. I sensed some did not want me to take the job because of bias and I was pondering whether to accept the job if it was offered. "You've got to take the job," Campy said. "It's not about you." I asked him what he meant, and he told me bluntly that it was about the kids—the high school and college students that would see me in that role.

This was an emotional turning point—it shook me up. I

realized he was right. I would be the first African American to hold this position in Kent County, the fourth largest county with the second largest city in the state of Michigan. My role in life was not to serve myself, but to serve others. And so, I accepted the position in the hope I would be able to help change some of the systems that thwart opportunity for the disenfranchised in our community and that young people would look at me and believe they also could be leaders.

It was the help of others—Black and White—who gave me the opportunity to build a successful career. One turning point for me came when I received a scholarship to attend a multi-day Boy Scouts camp while I was a boy in North Carolina. It was an experience that enabled me to visualize a larger world and a better future. Scouting helped me to understand the importance of self-reliance, initiative, courage, helpfulness, integrity, sportsmanship, and resourcefulness.

I wanted today's disadvantaged youngsters to have the same chance. So, when I was president of the Boy Scouts' Gerald R. Ford Field Service Council and learned that our Michigan Crossroads Council was discussing plans to sell our building near Grand Rapids, I argued vehemently that we should keep it and went to work pulling together community resources to keep it going and make it better than ever.

Over the course of two-and-a-half years, we raised $6.2 million to upgrade the DeVos Family Center for Scouting in the city of Walker, just five miles from downtown Grand Rapids. And we expanded the property to 37 acres and created what is now called Adventure Point, with programs that emphasize experiential learning. The hands-on activities for boys and girls revolve around team building, leadership, sustainability and STEM (Science, Technology, Engineering and Mathematics). There are also plenty of opportunities for what the Scouts call COPE—Challenging Outdoor Personal Experience. COPE includes the development of individual skills as well as group challenges to perform activities such as climb, swing, balance, jump, rappel and problem-solve. Scholarships help young people from impoverished backgrounds to experience activities at Adventure Point.

I leveraged my role as administrator of Kent County to help bring people together to get things done. Making our community more prosperous for the benefit of those less fortunate was an important priority. It's a role that often requires sacrificing ego and setting aside biases against people because of their politics. The reality is that there are many needs that require financial investment to address. If the African American community doesn't have enough money, where do we go? It makes sense to me to go to where the money is to provide the resources needed to improve lives, and that often means the White community.

I also believe that we African Americans need to self-reflect on how we can be more effective in designing ways to improve conditions. Sometimes we can be our own worst enemy and not see our potential and the things that we ourselves need to change and appreciate. I must ask myself, "What do I need to do? How much time do I spend developing my acumen and my ability to more effectively communicate my ideas? How can I plan better, organize better, to elicit the response that I need from those who can help? How can I ensure that I am at the right place at the right time, and how do I grow my credibility to make change happen?" These aren't all racial issues. Sometimes it comes down to individual people issues and the things that we can control.

However, racism exists in every community and it keeps us from being the truly "United" States that we could be. All of our citizens should have a part to play in making America great. We need to wake up to what is possible in America and what it would take to clear the obstacles to every person realizing their potential. We need to wake up and act with urgency to make it happen.

And so, I look at Jon Lockard's painting every day, and I say to myself that I have an obligation to leverage my assets in order to help make the systemic and structural changes that will put young African Americans in a better position than I was in as a child growing up in America.

To the question, "What Will You Tell Them?", I want to say: I understand the rejection you sometimes feel.

But never forget that God loves you and that your life has purpose and value.

Despite the rejection you may sometimes feel or the obstacles you may face, your life has purpose and meaning, and you can build a successful life.

And when the torch is passed to your generation, I want you to continue to bend the arc of history toward the fulfilment of your potential.

CHAPTER 7

Continuous Improvement

The average NBA career is less than five years. When I was pursuing a spot in pro basketball during the late 1970s, the sport was nowhere near as popular as it is today—in fact, the 1978 and 1979 NBA finals were actually televised on tape delay instead of live. Only a few players made large salaries, and I knew I needed to have a plan for life after the hardwood. I didn't want to look back one day and regretfully ask myself, "What do I have?"

So, in early 1978 when Grand Rapids-based Steelcase offered me the chance to come on board in a management training program, it made sense to begin charting a new course. NBA roster decisions were often political and my chance for a long run was a crapshoot. My first daughter, Raven Nicole, had recently been born and I didn't want to put the family through uncertainties. And as my oldest brother Alonza once shared with me that my grandma Vida liked to say, "A bird in the hand is better than ten in a bush"—in other words, appreciate the opportunities that were given me. This would be a chance to elevate my leadership capacity and have a career with longevity.

I ended up spending more than 24 years with Steelcase. I dealt with many challenges during this time and developed many new assets, both professionally and personally. Founded in 1912, Steelcase is the largest office-furniture manufacturer in the world. During the 1970s and 1980s when I was with the company, it was expanding internationally into Asia, Europe and North Africa. The company prospered over the years by adapting to an ever-changing workplace and coming up with innovative and ergonomic designs.

I was one of the first management trainees in Steelcase's Professional Accelerated Career Entry (PACE) program that was intended to develop key future leaders of the organization. I was also the first African American in PACE, and some folks at the company didn't see me as becoming a leader. It wasn't always easy to make it work, but I overcame those prejudices to make my mark.

As part of the training, we spent time with various departments to learn what they did. We would write up reports about our experience and what improvements might be made, then rotate to another department on the way to getting placed in a management position. I had a choice to go into sales and marketing, or human resources and employee relations. To the displeasure of Paul Witting, the VP for sales, I chose human resources and employee relations after talking with Jack Spalding the head of human resources. I originally was slated to work in sales and marketing. My first management assignment was in the Desk Plant, becoming the first assistant employee relations manager at that location. I was later promoted and established the employee relations office for the company's Shipping and Distribution division. After working in several other facilities, I became senior employee relations manager and headed up all night shift employee relations for the company.

I had to wear two hats as an employee relations manager. One role involved the reality that I was in support to management. At the same time, my job included being an intermediary and advocate for employees who helped them and managers better understand each other and resolve conflicts. I saw disparities in the way people were treated, including some situations that related to racial or gender bias. I saw the need to have someone advocating for change, because otherwise people typically just continue to do what they're doing.

The experience reinforced my desire to get in a position to shake up the status quo, and to inspire and motivate people to reach their full potential. I was heavily influenced by Wayne Alderson's philosophy of valuing people and value of the person as detailed in the book, *Stronger Than Steel* by R.C. Sproul. The book tells of how Alderson led the turnaround at Pittron Steel by getting management and the labor unions to work together through love-dignity-respect. He was a coal miner's son who became a corporate executive and an advocate of positive labor-management relations by developing Christian trust and responsiveness among workers and executives. His life mirrored much of my belief system and what I had learned growing up on the farm in North Carolina. Wayne visited me once when I was Steelcase Systems Furniture 1 Plant employer relations manager. I attempted to convince the senior VP of manufacturing at the time to endorse and promote the Value of the Person theory, but to no avail. It was a pivotal moment for me in understanding culture and how difficult it was to change it.

One morning at the Systems 1 Plant, Bob Ballard, who became president of North American operations at Steelcase, came into the facility soon after his appointment to begin conducting baseline surveys for all manufacturing plants. It was before 6 a.m., and he was surprised to find me there. "What are you doing here?", he asked. "We don't typically see human resources people in the plant this early in the morning." Ballard asked me what I wanted to do with the company, and I replied that one day I wanted to be in leadership. "Oh, okay," he replied. A seed had been planted.

A few months later I was in a meeting led by Ballard at the seven-story Pyramid building, the corporate design center at the time. As I sat there with other employee relations managers from around the country, Ballard announced that he wanted me to take a position as a supervisor at the Panel Plant. Some of the people in the room smirked and laughed at the notion because it would have been a step down in the organization, but Ballard assured them he was serious. He evidently saw the value of my becoming one of the leaders of the organization. Operations management was the track he wanted me to go through.

After I arrived at the Panel Plant, Steelcase decided to make a significant change in its production process by implementing a world-class manufacturing system. Based on lean-manufacturing principles, the system's goal is to eliminate waste by continuously improving efficiency in a systematic and organized way. People need to buy in to make it work. World-class manufacturing requires the participation of everyone, at every level. Working in teams, workers are engaged in planning, execution and problem solving.

I was part of a team that studied and benchmarked other major companies that had put world-class manufacturing into place in their own operations. We visited the New United Motor Manufacturing, Inc. (NUMMI) in Fremont, California, which was jointly owned by Toyota and General Motors; the assembly plant for GM subsidiary Saturn in Spring Hill, Tennessee; and Cargill, a global leader in agriculture based in Wayzata, Minnesota. We spoke to leaders, observed operations and evaluated how they treated their people. World-class manufacturing uses thorough processes to set priorities and implement improvement in many areas such as safety, quality, ergonomics, logistics and maintenance.

The most important thing I learned is that people are ultimately the vital link. It's not the machines, it's not the equipment, it's the people. At its heart, world-class manufacturing is based on empowering workers to use their experience and know-how. Team members understand that they have a leading role to play in improving their areas of work.

"Kaizen," a Japanese term that means "continuous improvement," is an action plan that uses the principles of world-class manufacturing. The first kaizen at Steelcase took place in my department, which machined and welded standard and special parts for office panel partitions for the company. Along with my boss Tom Allsberry and plant manager Bruce Mclenithan, I was at the tip of the spear to change how the company operated. There was a lot riding on our ability to succeed so that the rest of the company could proceed confidently to execute world-class manufacturing.

We had a target of two weeks to complete the initial project, which involved reducing floor space while increasing throughput. Before the kaizen, a lot of room was taken up by excess parts that were stacked up high. When the parts were finally pulled out for production, it turned out they were often defective.

Our kaizen reduced inventory by 50%, condensed floor space by 25% and increased throughput by 30%. And it kicked off a transitional change for the company, moving toward a Just-in-Time (JIT) inventory system that is a cornerstone of lean manufacturing. JIT, which is one aspect of world-class manufacturing, basically means aligning material orders with production schedules. It aims to make only what customers want, with shorter lead times. Every department in the Panel Plant was linked together in a cohesive rhythm in order to eliminate the waste of excess raw material and finished inventory that was not ready to go to market.

When many individuals continuously make small improvements to their own areas, the end result is a flood of progress. But to reach this ultimate goal, we needed to get the support of employees. Workers were not used to doing things this new way, and they were wary of management's intentions. I knew we had to prove that we really listened to them and valued their input. We involved them in the redesign of the department layout, meeting regularly with them to getting their feedback on that and on other issues that were put on the table.

One young woman in the department, Diane, was vigorously opposed to the change. She was in an area with a piecework arrangement, where employees earned pay based on how many units they produced. It sounds like a reasonable concept, but it has some major drawbacks because an employee focusing on quantity might cut corners on quality, equipment maintenance or safety. It also puts the focus on an individual instead of the team's ability to deliver high-quality products in an efficient and timely manner.

Diane vented her complaint about the change to plant manager Bruce McClenithan and to Bob Ballard, North America Operations president. I was notified and told I needed to make it work. My first reaction was that we should be disciplining her for cheating the system by stacking parts. But instead, my assistant supervisor Eric Spearman and I worked to help her move forward and connect to the team.

I realized it was important to her to feel valued. McClenithan liked to reward workers by sending a rolling popcorn machine around to a department to celebrate whenever the group hit 100% schedule completion. One day, when the cart was in my department, I told Eric to fill a bag and give it to Diane. He wondered why, and I told him we had to get her back on board. So he did that. She was astonished. It flipped a switch. Diane said she couldn't believe what we had done, and she became my number one supporter from that time onward.

I learned a great deal from the choice to deal with her in a constructive manner. Small gestures of appreciation matter to people. I could have done things by the book and disciplined her, but I realized that change impacts people in different ways. As a leader, you need to work with what you've got. You can't punish people to the point where they disengage and won't become part of the solution. This young lady came back into the fold, became a solid team member, and we continued to improve. The department became one of the best.

I eventually was promoted to operations superintendent at the Context Plant. But before I left the Panel Plant, Diane and the rest of the team presented me with a plaque that named me "Number 1 Supervisor." It read: *"For Always Going Out of Your Way, And Doing The Extra Things That Make Our Work More Enjoyable and Productive"*. I really cherished that. I understood by then the importance of engineering the environment, so people are valued and appreciated. That is the path to building trust, and when trust is present, all the other stuff tends to work out. Workers know how to build things, how to fix things, and how to improve things. It's the relationships that unlock their potential and their capabilities. Once people realize that their ideas are welcome, their involvement spreads like wildfire.

At the Context Plant, I oversaw 200 employees and budget exceeding $60 million. Applying world-class manufacturing strategies, we implemented cost reductions averaging $2 million and achieved a 15% labor improvement for four consecutive years. The plant operating profit reached 31.7%, beating the goal of 25%.

One of the techniques we used to analyze and solve problems was called the 5 Whys method. It is a method that originated with the Toyota Production System's approach to lean manufacturing. The 5 Whys is designed to get at the root cause of any issue. Instead of jumping to a conclusion and applying a temporary bandage, you bring together those affected by the problem to take a deeper dive.

Sometimes people tend to only look at the surface level of a problem and they end up correcting a symptom rather than a cause. Repeatedly asking "why" is like peeling away the layers of an onion to expose the layers underneath. When you answer the first "why," it usually leads to another question. Asking "why" five times is a rule of thumb, but it might take fewer or more times before you get to the point of preventing future mistakes and failures. Discovering and then fixing the fundamental cause is the best way prevent future failures. The 5 Whys technique is a very effective tool for production teams to make an informed decision that improves performance.

Based on the progress made at the Context Plant and to further my growth and development, I was assigned to the role of performance management consultant for the corporate quality group. In this position I along with others looked at operations and recommended we use the Malcolm Baldridge Criteria for Performance Excellence to better evaluate operations.

The U.S. Congress established the Baldridge Program in 1987 to encourage companies to improve quality and business performance and raise awareness about the value of those attributes in gaining a competitive edge. The Baldridge Performance Excellence criteria provide a framework for organizations to improve overall performance. The principles are organized into seven categories: Leadership; Strategic Planning; Customer Focus; Measurement, Analysis, and Knowledge Management; Workforce Focus; Operations Focus; and Results.

I also helped develop the Steelcase Performance Excellence Strategy in alignment with the quality management principles established by the International Organization of Standards (ISO). We transitioned from ISO 9000/94 to ISO 9000/2001. ISO 9000 consists of a set of international standards on quality management and quality assurance developed to help companies effectively document the elements needed to maintain an efficient quality system.

These Steelcase experiences educated me a great deal in the art of leading people. I learned the importance of interacting effectively with others and I worked on managing my own stress instead of taking it out on someone else. I gained knowledge that it is more effective to develop trust rather than to use fear for motivation. And the experience drove home that it is critical to equip workers with the resources and freedom to improve safety, quality and efficiency in their own areas.

At one point during my time at Steelcase, I went to a high-level executive and asked him to mentor me. Helping others grow is a critical part of building a successful organization, and mentoring is key to developing the next generation of leaders. I believe key executives need to approach this task with a sense of mission. But to my surprise and disappointment, this executive told me that he did not mentor people. In later years, the same exec did mentor others. I couldn't help but wonder if his real message was, "We don't mentor Black people."

Overall, Steelcase had a reputation as a good place to work, and there was no union at the company. Competitive pay and benefits were factors, but employee relations were critical. Bob Pew was president of Steelcase when I joined and would later become chairman of the board. He had an open-door policy that encouraged communication and discussion about issues. One of Bob's maxims was, "You can't legislate productivity, you have to win the hearts and minds of the people." That set a tone that management was committed to considering the welfare of all workers in instigating policies and practices.

But the company could have done better dealing with diversity. I observed that Steelcase fell short in recruiting, hiring and promoting people of color, as well as women. There was some attempt to educate executives in the realities of personal and systemic biases, and its effects on employees. For example, all supervisors and managers in manufacturing were expected to attend a healing racism class. As part of the class, we watched a video that showed five guys sitting around a room with a facilitator to talk about issues.

The Black guy in the video gave a dissertation on what he felt was going on in his environment. He said he felt like he was swimming in shark-infested waters. That registered with me as I recognized I was like the man in the video. I could not contain myself and broke down in tears during class when I heard that. I felt that many people in the organization didn't embrace me like they accepted others who were also trying to ascend. There were double standards. I didn't let it undo me, but going through it was no piece of cake. I didn't always put on the table what I felt because I would get mocked or misunderstood. Or, worse, information would be used against me. I had to be careful as I tried to navigate the system.

I had moved beyond my years as an athlete, but it seemed like some people in management still looked at me as a jock. I didn't care for this, as I knew there is a fallacious stereotype that jocks are not bright. I was sometimes introduced as "Wayman Britt, he played basketball at the University of Michigan and for the Lakers and Pistons" instead of "Wayman Britt, he graduated from the University of Michigan and is one of our up-and-coming leaders." I didn't want people to think of me first and foremost as an athlete. During my time as employee relations manager, more than one plant executive told me to stop using "fancy words." What was I going to do? I felt like I had to dummy down in order to fit in.

I sometimes felt isolated because of the lack of networking and mentoring opportunities. One time, I went through a training program in which my classmates and I had to each verbalize our purpose. The other supervisors came up with a tag line to describe me: "Now you see him, now you don't." This pointed to the reality that I didn't engage with them after work, doing the things they liked doing. I often felt I was ostracized, belittled or mocked. But I realized from that assessment by others that I had to suck it up and move on. I made up my mind to risk engagement no matter what I was going through.

That was a big lesson for me. Instead of being negative, I had to move on and not let people get my goat. I learned to maintain a positive attitude, no matter what was going on. I made it a point to stay engaged.

I challenged one of my bosses over the fact that the company kept hiring from the outside to bring in managers into our group at a higher level than me. He told me to be thankful for where I was at, and mentioned another person, a vice president's son, who came in with me who hadn't reached a higher level. When I asserted that this was irrelevant because the co-worker who started with me had personal issues, my boss took offense. He became oppressive towards me after that. And I believe it was because I had challenged him and the good old boy system that had been playing out. But it only made me stronger and more resilient.

My 24 years with Steelcase turned out to be a time of great personal and career growth. At one point, when I was in the self-assessment training class, we were asked to reflect upon our lives, craft our purpose statement, and then share it with one another.

When my turn came to tell my purpose, I said it was "to serve others." This would be my north star going forward in life.

My Steelcase years were definitely a time of great growth in my understanding of how to be an effective leader. I came to see how to work with people, and learned a great deal about why people come to work and what's in it for them beyond a paycheck.

There were individuals who were willing to go the extra step to help me become successful. In other situations, I learned a lot through the necessity of persevering and nurturing my character. I brought all this knowledge and insight when I later went to work for Kent County government. So in the end, the challenges I overcame at Steelcase were a plus-plus-plus.

The following 16 pages are photos gathered from the life of Wayman Britt... so far.

Visits with Grandpa John and Grandma Annie Britt were very special for me. I remember how my Grandpa John used to affectionately pinch my cheeks and Grandma Annie always had molasses syrup ready to enjoy with buttermilk biscuits at the kitchen table when I was boy.

My mom Mamie (top left)), sister Joyce and dad Oscar pose soon after our move to Flint with two neighbor children (bottom two on the right) and three of my older sister Mert's children Bootsie (from left) Darnell and Buddy.

Aunt Alarce gave me great support, especially in my youth and later when I went through difficult personal challenges.

Brothers Jimmie (from left), Curt, Jay, Ray, and Alonza gathered at a family reunion.

Daddy, brother Ray and Uncle Paul enjoyed festivities at the Britt family reunion. Uncle Paul is the one who first got a job in an auto plant in Flint and urged us to move there.

School desegregation in North Carolina resulted in me being bused to Cleveland High School, where I became the first freshman and first Black player to start on the basketball team.

Flint Northern Basketball Coach Bill Frieder presented me a trophy that came with my being named an all-state player.

The 1973-74 Michigan team won the Big 10 championship and went on to play in the NCAA tournament.

Rising up for a jump shot in a game against Minnesota.

I was always pumped up to play against Ohio State, a big rivalry for Michigan.

Michigan Coach Johnny Orr was like a father figure to me and we maintained a relationship long after my basketball career.

The University of Michigan awarded me the Fielding H. Yost Award for "academic and athletic excellence."

At Michigan, I took on the challenge of guarding top scorers like Scott May of Indiana.

At Steelcase, I joined with other managers to head to the company's quarterly business meeting.

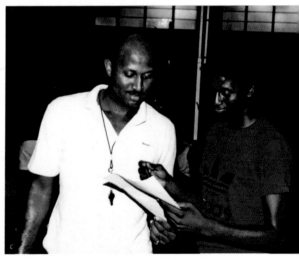

Son Eric and I go over some notes at the Leadership Basketball Camp I launched in 1986.

Brothers Curt (from left), Jay and Jimmie toured the Britt Family Yurt Village which houses overnight stays by Boy Scouts taking part in Adventure Point programs.

Daughter Ariel braving it on a hiking trek in Colorado. I am proud of her becoming associate director at the White House Office of National Drug Control Policy.

Dinah threw a surprise 50th birthday party after I came home from playing golf with my brothers-in-law.

One of my important duties as Kent County administrator/controller was to prepare the annual budget and present it to the Board of Commissioners.

Comedian Sinbad, a native of west Michigan, came to Grand Rapids to perform at Laughfest, a fundraiser for Gilda's Club which provides support programs for those living with cancer. Sinbad remembered me from my Michigan basketball days and when Dinah picked him up at the airport he called me up and we got together.

◄ Peter Secchia, former ambassador to Italy and a longtime friend of President Gerald Ford, was a driving force in the creation of the West Michigan Sports Commission.

Jack Harbaugh helped me launch the Adventure Point scholarship fund. Jack, a former college player and coach, is the father of U of M Coach Jim Harbaugh and Baltimore Ravens Coach John Harbaugh. Jack pinch-hit for son Jim at a West Michigan Sports Commission luncheon. He also hosted me and other family members on a tour of Schembechler Hall on the University of Michigan campus.
▼

I love all my kids and grandkids and enjoy celebrating special events like granddaughter Amiah's high school graduation.

Raven Nicole is my oldest daughter. As a 9-year-old, her note that she loved me lifted my spirits.

Celebrating my retirement as County Administrator/Controller was a joyous occasion. Celebrating with my wife Dinah, children, and grandchildren was icing on the cake.

University of Michigan Basketball Coach John Beilein spoke at a West Michigan Sports Commission luncheon and afterward joined me and Becky Bechler, managing partner at Public Affairs Associates.

Mike Melinn (center), Ray Davis and I were among the people associated with the Boy Scouts Michigan Crossroads Council who went on a backpacking trip in the mountains of New Mexico. The expedition inspired my idea to create Adventure Point on 37 acres near Grand Rapids with programs that provide experiential learning for scouts.

Thanks to the efforts of the President Ford Field Service Council's Scoutreach program, more young African Americans are on the way to becoming Eagle Scouts. Lee Moyer (left), Scoutreach VP; and Aaron Gach, field service council executive, join me in encouraging the aspirations of these Scouts.

Dinah and I joined artist Paul Collins who created the imagery behind us for an exhibit in the Kent County Administration Building commemorating the 50th anniversary of the assassination of Martin Luther King, Jr.

Friends Carol and David Van Andel, known for their community involvement and philanthropy, helped Dinah and me celebrate my retirement from Kent County.

Jim Hackett (left) and Greg Meyer joined me at the celebration for my 2021 retirement as administrator/controller of Kent County. Hackett was a colleague when I was at Steelcase and went on to become CEO of Steelcase and then Ford Motor Company. Meyer, a Grand Rapids native, won the Boston Marathon in 1983, and at the time of this event he served as chief community officer for Michigan Health-West.

Shortly after my retirement as administrator/controller of Kent County, the Greater Grand Rapids NAACP honored me with its Presidents Award. Dinah joined me during the presentation made by County Commissioner Robert Womack (left) and Cle Jackson, president of the NAACP chapter.

Former Michigan basketball teammate C.J. Kupec (with the "M" sweater), friend Jim Pike (far right) and I get ready to head out on the golf course for the 2021 Fulfilling the Dream Celebrity Open.

Among those enjoying the 2021 Fulfilling the Dream Celebrity Open are former University of Michigan athletes Phil Hubbard (from left), Hal Morris, C.J. Kupec, Tim Kuzma, me and Steve Grote.

⌐ CHAPTER 8 ⌐

Serving Others

Determining my purpose was a long process. It began when I was a young kid growing up in North Carolina and I prayed that I would be chosen to receive a scholarship to attend a Boy Scouts camp. The camp experience showed me that life offered more opportunities than I had ever conceived and it was a turning point in my journey.

This scholarship to camp was a great gift. As I matured, I continued to be blessed with chances that many others did not have. Teachers, coaches and family members encouraged my dreams. My Aunt Alarce, a beautician who lived in New Jersey, didn't have any kids of her own but she took an interest in me from the time I was a boy. She believed in me and reached out to offer support even when I went through troubled times as an adult.

Not everybody is lucky enough to have people who provide a lifeline in times of need. Many people—too many—live in poverty and neglect, and I came to understand that I had a responsibility to give back so they too could have hope for something better. I could not in good conscience be indifferent to those who need a hand up. I realized that shaping the world the way we want it to be is not something that can be delegated to others.

My mother lived a life of being kind and demanded that my siblings and I respect other people. Treat others as one would wish to be treated, she reminded us. This is the essence of the Golden Rule, which is common to religions around the world. Rushworth Kidder, who was an author and founder of the Institute for Global Ethics, said the concept exists in Christianity as well as Hinduism, Islam, Judaism and "the rest of the world's major religions."

Jesus, the greatest leader to have ever lived, took the notion even further. He washed the feet of his apostles, a truly humble thing to do. This act showed his love for his followers and left us an example of how serving others is part of the highest form of leadership.

The idea of serving others is also an essential part of some secular organization. The U.S. Air Force lists "service before self" as one of its three core values. As its handbook states, "If the leader is unwilling to sacrifice individual goals for the good of the unit, it's hard to convince others to do so." Similarly, the Rotary Club has adopted "service above self" as its motto, conveying its purpose of helping others through volunteer efforts.

When I first fully committed to making service to others central to my life, I launched the nonprofit Leadership Basketball Camp in 1986. The way I developed the resolve to begin that project is a story of how life offers opportunities for personal growth if we are open to seizing the chances presented to us.

I was a member of St. Philip's Episcopal Church in Grand Rapids. I became very involved, acting as president of the Men's Club, choir director and junior warden, which is the second lay leader. I was pretty good working with my hands, and one weekend I joined with others in the men's club to repair and renovate the church parish house. The rooms were in bad shape and the building lacked central heat. The rector of the church, Fr. Thomas Smith, and church secretary, Mrs. Hazel Grant, worked out of the garage that was heated with a portable heater. Over the weekend, Men's Club members repainted and remodeled that place, paved the parking lot, planted shrubs, put in a study for the pastor and an office for the secretary, and created a library.

I had been reading books on positive thinking, including *Time Enough to Win* by former Dallas Cowboys quarterback, Roger Staubach. In the book, Staubach went beyond talking about his playing career to call attention to his faith in Jesus. Another book was *Power for Living*, by Jamie Buckingham. I was beginning to sense that serving others was the path God was steering me to take.

One weekend, along with a few other leaders from our congregation, I attended a Cursillo Movement retreat at a nearby Roman Catholic parish. Cursillo is a Spanish word that means "short course." The Cursillo Movement was started in Spain by Catholic laymen, then grew around the world and opened up to those from other Christian denominations.

All of us attending the event stayed overnight and slept in bunk beds. The experience included two days of talks and discussions designed to nurture personal spiritual development while training laypeople to become effective Christian leaders by living and sharing their faith. Participants then take what they have learned back into the world, which the movement refers to as the Fourth Day. When the weekend ended, I was a changed man. It confirmed what I had been pondering about life, and what was important. That it wasn't about me. It was about serving, supporting, loving, and building other people up. But I didn't yet have a firm plan to begin implementing these objectives.

The week following the retreat, Bill Nickerson, another

Men's Club member at St. Philip's, gave me a book, *Go For It*, by Episcopalian minister Dr. John Guest. Bill said I should read this book about this guy who was doing outreach and ministering to young people—the same idea I had been talking about.

Born in Oxford, England, Dr. Guest came to the United States in 1964. Using his own musical ability, he formed a Christian contemporary music group to draw young people to meetings. He wrote about 30 books and took his outreach activities around the U.S. and to international destinations in Europe, Africa and Latin America. He loved working with young people, including those in Holland, Michigan which was only about 30 miles from Grand Rapids. His evangelistic crusades brought in a wide variety of people, including those in inner cities. Dr. Guest also made connections with business leaders, challenging executives to make a positive impact in their communities. The book I read by Dr. Guest stoked my passion. And soon, another opportunity to think about my mission in life presented itself.

One of the executives at Steelcase that I admired was Bob Pew. He was one of the owners and was the president of the company when I worked there. He had a heart for people, and his door was always open to employees who had questions or suggestions. We both belonged to Episcopalian churches in Grand Rapids – Bob at Grace, while I was part of St. Philip's congregation. He gave me $400 to attend a conference in Pittsburgh in the mid-1980s to help me grow my capacity to do outreach for the church in our community. The trip ended up being even more impactful than I could have imagined.

I went to Pittsburgh with Fr. Smith, the rector at St. Philip's. We stayed at the residence of Fr. Ben Winsor, a priest at St. Stephen's Episcopalian church. Thursday, a day before the final day of the conference, Fr. Winsor suggested we accompany him to nearby Sewickley, Pennsylvania, to see the church of another priest who had helped remodel and refurbish St. Stephen's. He said the priest there was an evangelist who went around the country reaching out to young people and converting them to Christ.

While we were visiting this beautiful church, we encountered a man in the lobby. To my amazement, it was Dr. Guest, the author of *Go For It*, the inspiring book that Bill Nickerson had given me to read. He invited us into his office, where I noticed photos on his wall of Lynn Swann and John Stallworth, two great Pittsburgh Steelers football players. During our time in the office, Fr. Guest also got a phone call from Gary Anderson, another Steelers player. My mind started turning. Wow, these current and former professional athletes are figuring out how they can help young people. So, okay—why couldn't I start a leadership camp for youth? I could invite some friends from my basketball days to come back and help.

Then Dr. Guest asked what we were doing the next day. He suggested we attend a Thank God It's Friday breakfast session in downtown Pittsburgh, where he would be co-leading the session with business leader Reid Carpenter. The TGIF group consisted of business leaders and church officials who came together to talk about how to live a Christian life in their management positions. We live in a society where it can be difficult for those in the executive ranks to reflect their faith in the way they lead their organizations. The pressure to deliver profits can distract managers from integrating their faith into their business practices. The TGIF group was a way to bring people together to talk about living their values.

I was intrigued. Instead of going to the workshop at the

conference, I decided it could be more fruitful to attend the meeting and hear Dr. Guest speak. He delivered a memorable talk about forgiving, forgetting and being free. That struck a chord with me because I was going through a very difficult time in my life, as my marriage to Marilyn was falling apart.

Dr. Guest spoke of the wounded hands of Jesus. He made the point that no matter what happens to you, no matter how hurt you are, no matter what people have done to you, you will never be as scarred, never be as beaten up as Christ was. Yet Jesus didn't let it stop Him from helping others. The message was clear: we should avoid whining and do something to help others.

When I boarded my flight in Pittsburgh to return to Grand Rapids, I could hardly believe who was sitting across the aisle from me. It was John Guest, who was on his way to speak to students at Calvin College, a Christian-based school in Grand Rapids. I told him about my vision to reach across the community to serve the needs of the kids growing up there.

Dr. Guest encouraged me to stand up in church and tell people my ideas. "What?" I replied. "I'm not a priest. I can't do that." But Fr. Smith was with us and he said it didn't matter that I wasn't ordained. He expressed full support for what I was talking about and said I could get up in church and tell people what was in my heart.

Clare DeGraaf, an important developer in town, picked up Dr. Guest when we landed in Grand Rapids. He was hosting the minister during his stay, and he drove me home. Dr. Guest was speaking at an event at Calvin College and he and DeGraaf invited me to attend. The event also featured a talk by Rosey Grier, a man of many talents and interests. A former star NFL football lineman, Grier had gone on to make a name as an actor, author and singer. He was at Robert F. Kennedy's side the night the senator was assassinated by Sirhan Sirhan during the 1968 presidential campaign, and it was Grier who wrestled the gun from the shooter to prevent further violence.

Grier got ordained as a Christian minister and became deeply involved in urban youth outreach programs. Grier helped start American Neighborhood Enterprises and its off-shoot, Impact Urban America. The objective of these organizations is to provide job training, employment and affordable housing to disadvantaged young people in inner cities. Grier also became a part of the Lead Like Jesus Movement, aimed at teaching people how to model Jesus' leadership techniques and live out their faith by serving others.

His talk to students stirred my emotions, and since he was also a former athlete I again thought about how I could make a difference. Afterward, I had the chance to meet Grier back-stage. It was a short but memorable encounter.

"How're you doing?", Grier asked.

"I'm doing great," I responded.

Grier: "Presence."

Me: "What?"

Grier: "Presence."

Me: "What do you mean?"

Grier: "You've got presence."

I interpreted the conversation as encouragement to be who I was and to follow the direction in which I was leaning. It was a very uplifting moment for me.

By the time Sunday came along, I had also been inspired by a note from our oldest daughter, Raven, who wrote that she loved me. It was the first time she had written a letter in cursive. I was on Cloud 9. Her letter filled with me joy, and affirmed the love for others and the importance of reaching our full potential that had begun to grow in my heart. Then, on Sunday morning, our daughter Tia was able to put our younger daughter Ean in her car seat for the first time. Tia was so excited about doing something she had never done before. I thought then that if she could do it, I could surely go to church and do something I had never done before.

So I went to church, and after the priest introduced me, I told the congregation that I believed my calling was to serve other people. I said I felt deep love and wanted to reach out to young people in the community and hoped church members would help in putting a basketball court on church property and starting a basketball camp. At one point a woman near the back of the church stood up and said, "Wayman, whatever you want to do, we're with you!"

All this encouragement bolstered my resolve and I oversaw the opening of the Leadership Basketball Camp at the former St. Joseph Seminary in Grand Rapids, which had a nice gym and rooms for overnight stays. I had maintained many relationships that had been formed during my basketball career, and now several of these contacts accepted my invitation to show up and help during the two summers that the camp was open. Those who volunteered their time included Johnny Orr, the former University of Michigan coach who had moved on to Iowa State; Bill Frieder, my Flint Northern High School coach who was now the head coach at Michigan; and my former Michigan teammates Campy Russell and Phil Hubbard, who both had gone on to have lengthy NBA careers.

Kids aged 9 to 14 attended, about a hundred each year. The first week was for the younger kids in camp, the second week for the older ones. It was boys-only the first year, but girls were included the second summer. I'm thrilled that some of those girls went on to form the core of some terrific basketball teams at Grand Rapids Ottawa Hills High School, including a squad that competed for the Michigan state basketball championship in 1989.

The camp wasn't just about basketball. The purpose went

beyond the skills development and games in order to encourage the youngsters to have a vision of becoming leaders. We gave talks about the importance of developing good character in order to be a leader. A local doctor spoke about how trees are only as strong as their roots. As people, our own roots need to be nourished in our formative years in order for us to live lives that are strong and grounded. Roots are not visible, but they provide the solid foundation we need to grow.

A few of the people who volunteered to help with the camp pushed me to rapidly expand it and make them paid staff. But we weren't ready to do that. I responded by referring to a baby rabbit I had recently seen. You can't ask baby rabbits to run until their legs are strong enough to run. Our camp was like a baby rabbit, it had to get stronger before we could run with it.

We never quite got to that point with the Leadership Basketball Camp. After two years, I gave up the camp because it consumed too much time. It broke my heart to end it, but my job at Steelcase was too full and I was also dealing with marital issues that were draining my energy.

About the time that the camp closed, I was obligated to attend a conference in Kansas City with my immediate boss. On the plane, I talked with a young man from Liberty University who was doing a Bible study. He was headed to Kansas City to lead a Bible Bowl event. The Bible Bowl is a quiz program in which student teams compete over their knowledge of a selected book of scripture. Teams compete in different age divisions.

After landing and heading to the luggage carousel, I was approached by another man who had been on the flight. He introduced himself as the pastor of a local church. He had evidently observed me discussing scripture with the student on the plane, and the pastor and I struck up a conversation.

Before we parted, he invited me to visit his church for a service on Sunday.

I took him up on the offer, which meant not meeting my boss and his wife for lunch. My boss was angry. I had previously challenged him on why outsiders had been brought in for positions higher than mine, and here he thought I was pouring gasoline on the fire because I wouldn't relegate myself to his wishes. But I felt it was important to visit the church, as I had been thinking a great deal about the direction of my life. The decision to not dine with my boss was not going to help my career. But making money at a job was seeming less urgent as I plotted out how to accomplish my mission to serve others. When I arrived at the church, Sunday school was going on before the service. Lo and behold, the class was discussing the same part of scripture that the young man on the plane had been talking about as the basis for the Bible Bowl he was going to lead.

After service the pastor asked me to go to his car and retrieve some papers. When I did so, astonishingly a pet rabbit was in a cage in the back seat of his car. I then reflected upon the analogy I had shared with my Leadership Camp staff about not pushing the camp too fast—that it had to get stronger before we could hit our stride and run faster. It was also an affirmation that I had to get stronger spiritually to run toward this new path for my life.

That day I also went with the pastor to see the property where he was overseeing the building of a new church. The site happened to be in a field of sunflowers. With its round face and yellow petals that remind us of sunshine, the sunflower is a symbol of loyalty, devotion and joy in many places around the world.

When I returned home from the trip, I was wondering if my calling was to become a minister. Dr. Guest actually offered to pay my educational expenses to get ordained. Contemplating this move, I sought the counsel of Bishop William Abney and Pastor Clifton Rhoades, two church officials in Grand Rapids whom I respected. I wanted to know if I was being called into the ministry.

Their message was that we didn't need any more preachers. The world needed men of God who were willing to serve others and who were capable of getting things done, and they said I was in the best place to do that with my career at Steelcase and background from the University of Michigan. They said God wanted me to use my assets and I had the perfect platform. Just serve.

I knew I had an ability to connect with people. I could use that skill to encourage people to be all they could be and help fashion a better world. The challenge ahead was to constantly search for innovative ways to make the community a better place.

- CHAPTER 9 -

Never Give Up

Success is failure turned inside out –
The silver tint of the clouds of doubt,
And when you never can tell how close you are,
It may be near when it seems afar,
So stick to the fight when you're hardest hit –
It's when things go wrong that you mustn't quit.

These words are part of a poem written by Edgar Albert Guest. My Aunt Alarce sent me a card with the poem when I was going through marital troubles that ended in divorce. Through life, all of us suffer losses, some minor and others that can feel devastating. I am no exception to this reality of the human experience. Sometimes setbacks leave us feeling demoralized and we disconnect from much of the world. In times of adversity, we need to find a source of resilience in order to rebuild our lives.

My unsuccessful effort to build an NBA career was a disappointment, and for years I wondered if I had made the right choice to give up that dream and accept entry into a leadership training program with Steelcase. I had married Marilyn soon after college and we were building a life together, and I eventually concluded I had made the right choice in careers. But after years of marriage, and the birth of four beautiful daughters, we were drifting apart.

There are no winners playing the blame game in a divorce and I know the failure of our marriage was partly my fault. Perhaps the stress of my evolving life mission—embracing Christ's example to serve others—was a factor. Being competitive had driven me when I was an athlete, but now my focus had shifted to creatively doing whatever I could to improve society by helping lift up people who were disadvantaged. My decision to start the Leadership Basketball Camp underlined the fact that my life's journey had changed direction. I had come to understand myself as a person, and I was on a path of service.

Unanticipated change by a partner can be hard to accept, and I was certainly evolving as a person. I closed the basketball camp after two years, in part because of Steelcase work requirements, and also because of the stress at home. That was about when my wife filed for separation and eventually divorce. I had modeled myself after Julius Erving, "Dr. J," the great basketball player who seemed to embody the All-American guy with the All-American family. He appeared to have an ideal marriage, but then some years after my divorce, Dr. J's marriage also broke up.

After the legal filing for separation, I remained hopeful for some time that we could work things out. I knew then that I needed to move on, but it was still difficult to do. The pressure was so strong, others began to notice how troubled I was. Jim Soule, my boss' boss, asked me into his office one day. He was the Steelcase vice president of human resources, and a psychologist by training. I had no idea why he called me in. "Wayman, I want to talk to you about your marriage," he said. "You've got to let it go." I asked him why he would give me that advice. He responded, "It will grind you to a point where you can't function and buying a bunch of stuff won't fix it." This was another voice telling me to move on.

One night I had a dream in which a spirit, perhaps God, said to me that I needed to get rid of the "guilts." According to the spirit, if I didn't get rid of the guilts, they would kill me. And then I was shown a fireplace, and lined in the wall of the hearth there were many scarlet-red leech-like figures that were called guilts. Next, a big black truck appeared, as if straight out of the tobacco farm where I grew up. It was the kind of truck my father owned, on which we loaded things like baled hay or bags of potatoes. The truck rolled up to the back of the house, and the spirit said that if I didn't get rid of the guilts, I wouldn't be able to move on. The message was to not wallow in the guilt and disappointment I was feeling. Then I woke up.

The thought of not living with my daughters was painful. I went to counseling, sought spiritual advice from different pastors, and read books in an attempt to understand what I should do. I finally grasped that staying on, expecting things to get better, was not being realistic. I understood it was best to move on. But I was trying to figure out where to go. We had accumulated a lot of debt. I irrationally thought spending money on things like a new house, new car, big new television and other expensive possessions could help save the relationship. Eventually, we were forced to sell the house early and take a big loss because of the bills that were continuing to accumulate after we separated.

We had racked up so many bills that when I first left the home I had to sleep at the local YMCA. I was a senior employee relations manager at Steelcase, at the top of my work game, but here I was staying at a shelter where the homeless go. Steelcase gave me a loan that helped me get back on my feet in a financial way.

I finally found an apartment, on Blossom Street in Grand Rapids. I hoped that being on Blossom Street meant I was meant to start over and bloom where I was now planted. I believe God has a way of moving people where he wants them to be—that no matter what, He has a purpose for our lives. We need to just accept the heartaches and setbacks that we consider to be failures and embrace the fact that God still loves us and has a plan for us.

While I was living in the apartment on Blossom Street and going through the divorce, I met Dinah who helped my healing process. The story of how we connected is an example of how opportunities for change and growth can arise from encounters that might seem incidental at the time.

In 1973, when I played for Michigan, we went to Los Angeles for a basketball game against defending national champion UCLA. A couple of Michigan fans—Moe Rison and Michael Eanes—traveled to the game at Pauley Pavilion. Moe turned out to be a distant cousin of mine, and he was also the uncle of Andre Rison, a star football wide receiver at Flint Northwestern High School and Michigan State who ended up being a Pro Bowl player in the NFL. Moe and Mike visited us at our hotel when we were there.

Fast forward to 1987, and I was putting together a basketball team to play in a charity tournament taking place at Ottawa Hills High School in Grand Rapids. Among the guys who agreed to play were Phil Hubbard, a former Michigan teammate and my road roommate, and Walker D. Russell, brother of my college teammate Campy Russell. Phil and Walker both had begun good NBA careers and had helped at my Leadership Basketball Camp.

To support the charity, I approached some local businesses for contributions. Mike Eanes owned the Wolverine Fruit Garden on Division Street in Grand Rapids. "Don't I know you?", I asked when I saw Mike at his store. He reminded me that we had met in California. We got to talking, he agreed to contribute to the cause, and he invited me to come over to his home the day of the game so we would go together to the high school.

When I arrived at his house before the game, Mike asked if

it was okay for his aunt to come with us. That's when he introduced me to his Aunt Dinah, who was in the living room. After the game, we all went to a get a bite to eat at a nearby Big Boy restaurant. We finished about 10 o'clock that night and unfortunately, when we went back into the parking lot, I discovered someone had shot out my car window with a BB gun.

Phil needed to get back to his car to return to Cleveland where he was part of the Cavaliers team. So I suggested to Mike that he drive Phil to pick up his car while I cleaned out my auto. Dinah said she would stay and help. It was the first time I saw her spirit of helping and supporting. After I got back to my apartment we talked on the phone like we were long-lost soulmates until 3 a.m.

The next day, a Sunday, Mike invited me back to his house for a barbecue. Dinah was wearing the same mosaic colors as I was wearing. Although I still longed for my family, I felt God was telling me to start paying attention to her and that it was okay to think about someone else.

I learned that Dinah had two kids, Ron and Dee Dee, and she loved the Lord. Dinah worked for Zondervan, a Christian media and publishing company located in Grand Rapids. As part of her job, she accompanied Ben Carson on a tour to promote his first book, *Gifted Hands: The Ben Carson Story*. Ben is a retired neurosurgeon who ran for president in the 2016 primaries and later served as U.S. Secretary of Housing and Urban Development. Dinah and I are now friends with Ben and his wife Candy and we have hosted Ben at our home and also visited them.

During the time Dinah and I were getting to know each other, she gave me a wonderful book written by Betty Malz entitled *Angels Watching Over Me*. In the book, Christians share inspirational stories of receiving divine help with their lives. It is a testament to how the Lord cares for all of his children. In addition to the stories, there was another aspect of the book that caught my eye. The back cover of the book showed a lady with a collie—and in the background, there were sunflowers. This was the third time I had encountered sunflowers, following my visit to church property in Kansas City and then the visit to the farm where my accountant lived. It felt like things were coming together.

Dinah played a vital part in helping me turn my ship to sail much smoother. Her supportiveness and committed attitude has helped me to be me, and to fulfill my mission of serving others. Like me, she comes from a large family and understands the importance of listening, communicating and working as a team. Growing up in a Christian home, she knows God is looking for us to do our best.

I eventually asked Dinah to marry me, and I was overjoyed when she accepted. She is a wonderful companion. As my wife, Dinah's self-esteem and confidence has allowed me to move forward in life and follow my mission of helping others become successful.

A few days after Dinah and I wedded, my mom passed away. A poster with the quote, "Love is like a butterfly. It goes wherever it pleases and pleases wherever it goes" is one of the prized possessions I kept from her belongings when she died.

This poster reminds me that we all need love. "Knowledge puffs up, but love builds up," wrote St. Paul in his first letter to the Corinthians. Knowledge without love is prideful arrogance, but knowledge combined with love leads to humility. At that time of my life, I was coming to realize that we must light the world with love in even the little things we do. I believe there is hope in the world because God loves and forgives us, and this obliges us to find commonality with each other. Carrying anger or hatred weighs us down. Forgiving and forgetting is the way to be free.

Throughout life, we all make mistakes but the important thing is to learn from them. That learning starts with admitting where you went wrong and then approaching the situation as an opportunity to grow.

My daughter Ariel is a wonderful example of learning and growing from mistakes, and I am so proud of her. Ariel's life took a wrong turn as a teenager before she went on a journey of self-discovery. She started using drugs and alcohol before graduating from high school and her substance abuse continued when she began attending the University of Michigan. After dropping out, she headed to New York, but finally went into a recovery program and turned her life around. She returned to Michigan for her bachelor's degree in psychology and master's degree in social work.

Ariel found a sense of purpose, taking the lessons she learned in her life and working in areas of intervention and recovery for substance abusers. She became senior director of a Denver-based program to assist college students in recovery. In 2015, she was invited to share her personal recovery story at the White House as part of a panel sponsored by the Office of National Drug Control Policy. And then in 2021, she joined the Biden Administration as associate director at the White House Office of National Drug Control Policy.

Just about everybody sometimes reaches a point of wanting to give up. Changing this mindset is not easy. But just as my Aunt Alarce advised me, a lot of good can happen when you refuse to quit.

Often, it takes time to see the results of our commitment to move forward. I want to share a story about a man who was so demoralized that he wanted to quit his life. Before ending everything, the man decided to go into the woods to have a last talk with God.

"God," he asked. "Can you give me a single reason not to quit?"

God smiled and started narrating a wonderful story about a gardener.

The gardener planted seeds of bamboos and ferns in an empty plot of land. He took care of it by daily watering the seeds. One day he was delighted to see that the fern seeds had sprouted and within a few days it grew really fast into a beautiful fern bush. But nothing came out of the bamboo seed. Nonetheless, he kept watering it daily.

Even after one year, there was no sign of any growth from the bamboo seed. The gardener did not quit, even though the second year, and the third year, and then the fourth year passed with no sign of any growth.

Then it was the fifth year. One day the gardener finally spied a tiny shoot emerging from the soil. Then he was astounded to see that within the next six months the little shoot grew into a 60-foot bamboo plant.

"Do you know what really happened in those four years?", God asked. He went on to explain that the gardener's efforts of the first four years were not a waste of time and effort, despite what the outside world might have thought. Below the soil, away from the gardener's sight, the bamboo seeds developed roots and expanded below the surface. This created the strength for fast and sustained growth once the bamboo sprouted.

God then said, "My child, life is not a uniform flow and there will be ups and downs. Be patient and persistent. Don't compare yourself to short-term quick achievers who grow fast like the fern. Not everyone achieves success quickly. Remember that everyone has their own pace of progress. Your struggling or setbacks are temporary and are actually the building blocks to increase your resilience and propel you to greater and sustained success."

The man understood the lesson. He left the forest and brought back the story as a reminder to everyone that we should persist, because God will never abandon us. I am thankful I learned through my darkest times that God was preparing me for something bigger than I had imagined.

That is why we should never give up and let life's setbacks or guilt cripple us.

‑ CHAPTER 10 ‑

Taking It to the Next Level

A recession stalled the United States economy beginning in 2001, leading many companies to furlough some of their workers. Steelcase was one of those companies affected by the downturn, which began when the tech stocks bubble burst and accelerated with the September 11, 2001 terrorist attacks. Steelcase's sales and earnings decreased and the company decided to "rightsize," which is a euphemism for laying off employees. I was one of those let go by Steelcase in 2001, after working more than 24 years for the company.

Losing a job can be a devastating psychological and financial trauma. One colleague who was a popular and successful superintendent at Steelcase lost his job at the same time as me. Sadly, he went home and committed suicide.

I did not feel like the job was my life, and I was somewhat prepared for the possibility of being let go. Two vice-presidents had given me conflicting advice about my desire to take on a greater leadership role. One said I should have a greater sense of urgency, while a second one advised me I was being too aggressive in wanting to move up. It was hard for me to dial into what the best approach should be.

In addition, a couple of months earlier I had seen a comedy routine by the entertainer Steve Harvey. In his sketch, he joked about how White people seem to always be surprised when they are fired. But when cutbacks are being made, Black people figure "we will be first—and we can see it coming." It's the kind of joke that makes you want to laugh because of the humor, but maybe you want to cry too because it expresses the truth.

As a young man I had been cut by the Los Angeles Lakers and the Detroit Pistons, so I had learned to accept the fact that sometimes a job just doesn't work out the way I hoped. And I believed God still had a plan for me. By the time I left Steelcase, I didn't feel like the plan necessarily involved me being with that company forever. Losing the job released me to do some other things I wanted to pursue, such as try radio and television work to make use of skills I had learned at the University of Michigan. Along with my new friend Frank Moore, I had been producing a show called "Pure Gospel." Dinah was also working on production of the show and it gave me a chance to get to know her early in our relationship.

I also had some experience in carpentry and had been trying to improve my skills in that area. I started my own general contracting business to remodel homes and other structures, including our church. I would come home wearing my boots and other construction clothing and gear. Often I was tired, not just from deconstructing buildings and putting them back together, but also from dealing with some of the workers we brought in. I began thinking this was not the right fit. My wife Dinah urged me to start looking for other opportunities.

Right after I left Steelcase, I went through a career assessment conducted by Right Management, an outplacement consultancy. Steelcase made this a part of my separation agreement. The evaluators came back to me and said I had a proclivity for finance and human services work. My profile said these were the areas I should pursue—not working in manufacturing, but working with people, financial environments and with budgets. The idea of working with budgets had not entered my mind, since I didn't particularly like math in school. It turns out that didn't matter. Budgeting wasn't fundamentally about the arithmetic. It was more about how you create plans and execute strategies to get things done.

The Right Management evaluation opened me up to seeking some positions I might not have previously considered, including some in government. I began searching web sites for job postings. I saw the State of Michigan was looking for a director of the Department of Human Services and applied for that, but never heard back. There was a job opening for a deputy administrator of a county in North Carolina, the state where I grew up. Again, I applied but never got a response.

Then Kent County Deputy Administrator Alan Vanderberg left to become administrator for neighboring Ottawa County. Kent County is the fourth-largest county in Michigan and includes Grand Rapids, which has a population of about 200,000, and other cities and townships in the southwest part of Michigan. I decided to apply for the Kent County assistant administrator opening but thought I was a long shot to even get a call to interview.

However, I had gained experience with some boards and commissions in the area, and that must have helped my chances. My Steelcase boss Cal Jeter, whose background included working with Catholic Social Services, had urged those of us in employee relations to get involved in community service. Among my activities in Kent County, I served as a board member of the Grand Rapids Center for Environmental Studies, the Grand Rapids School of Bible and Music, and the Job Corps Community Relations Council. Job Corps is a U.S. Department of Labor program that provides free education and vocational training to young men and women, while also helping them with social and employability skills. The Job Corps interacted with a lot of schools and some of the non-profit organizations in the area. This experience gave me a base to understand how we needed to work together to solve problems in the community.

The Job Corps Community Relations Council included members from the Kent County Department of Human Services, and my involvement caught the eye of Evert Vermeer, the DHS director. He observed how I worked with other members of the Job Corps Community Relations Council and suggested that I apply to become a member of the DHS board. He pointed out that the Republican Party controlled the appointments that were made by the Board of Commissioners at the time, and urged me to become a member of the county's GOP 400 Club.

I didn't know anything about being a Republican or a Democrat. In 1993, the two parties were nowhere near as polarized as they are today, when it sometimes seems that everyone hates each other. There is so much finger-pointing and it is nearly impossible to get consensus on what to do. Over the years I have been criticized for being open to working with people of any political outlook, but I won't apologize for trying to work with everyone and bring people together.

I wanted to be part of making my community better and helping disadvantaged young people. If I had to join a political party to have influence to accomplish those goals, then that's what I would do. So I joined the 400 Club and went to the Kent County Lincoln Day dinner, hoping it would give me a better shot at getting on the DHS board. One person I encountered at the dinner asked me, "What are you doing here?" She and others weren't used to seeing African Americans at Republican events like this.

I did end up being appointed to the board of the Department of Human Resources, and eventually became chairman. The local state agency administers assistance for needy families, including medical, disability, food stamps and emergency relief programs, as well as child abuse, neglect and foster care services. Serving on the DHS board, I learned more about the plight of many residents in the community. With the encouragement of Ev Vermeer, I wrote a letter to the county administrator at the time, Dick Platte, saying that Kent County really needed to diversify the people who helped make decisions about priorities. He asked me to meet him and later asked that I join him and others to further assess the situation. This eventually led to their adding a manager to strengthen diversity and inclusion at Kent County.

Perhaps my involvement with county boards as well as my management experience at Steelcase—an important employer in the region—convinced county officials to invite me to interview for the deputy administrator position.

Several government officials from the county and managers from local municipalities were involved in the interviewing process, including County Administrator Daryl Delabbio, Sheriff Larry Stelma and Board of Commissioners Chairman David Morren. In the end, it came down to six candidates. I was the only one whose job experience was all in the private sector instead of government.

Yet in some important ways, the job was made to order for my qualifications. Kent County had recently begun establishing a performance measurement program. That was up my alley, because at Steelcase I had been part of an internal consultancy group that evaluated facilities and departments based on lean manufacturing principles and the national Malcolm Baldridge criteria to improve an organization's quality and performance. I had also saved dollars and improved quality by helping implement the first kaizen as the company moved to a world-class manufacturing system.

The county search committee also wanted someone with the ability to work with people, build strong teams and resolve conflicts. These were things that I had learned playing high-level basketball and working in employee relations at Steelcase. I gained experience at Steelcase helping dysfunctional teams—line workers, superintendents, plant managers—to deal with their issues and go forward in a better direction. I got great joy and satisfaction in solving people issues. I figured I could do an even better job if I had a chance to play a bigger role in an organization.

I went through my problem solving techniques in the interview. I knew the science of it from practical day-to-day learning and becoming certified in interaction management techniques. A lot of people in county governments lacked experience in successfully dealing with people issues, and in the end every organization succeeds or fails based on its people. At Steelcase, I had been required to rectify breached relationships. I had to figure out how to confront bad behavior, including alcohol and drug abuse problems. I learned how to best convince substance abusers to accept support, and how to deal with them if they won't try to change.

Morren asked me how I would handle a bad-behaving county commissioner who challenged him as the board chairman. I explained how I would help deal with a conflict like this if I became assistant administrator, based on my learnings of interaction management. I knew how to tell people what they needed to know in a way they could receive it. I had the ability to step on their shoes without them losing their shine. The goal is to build a person's self-esteem and yet still have the conversation that needs to be had. I used my knowledge of that process to explain in the interview how I would deal with that unruly commissioner without getting pulled into politics or undermining the chairman.

Years later Morren shared with me that after the interview, he said to Delabbio, "That's the guy. You need to hire him." I don't know if Delabbio was as high as Morren was on hiring me at first, but I think over the years he grew to like me. We met for lunch and he offered me the position. I told him I hoped for his mentorship since I had so little background in county government, but he told me that he couldn't mentor me, and I guess it was because of our soon-to-be manager/ subordinate relationship. He also let me know that his other assistant administrator would be Number One in the pecking order and I would have to be Number Two. I told him I had no problem with it, I just wanted to do the job.

In March 2004, Delabbio announced my hiring as assistant administrator for Kent County. I had already committed my life to serving others in ways that would empower them to achieve their God-given potential. I would now be in a position to take my mission to another level.

~ CHAPTER 11 ~

Performance Management

I needed to learn fast as I began my new job as assistant administrator for Kent County. During my first week, I spent most of my time reading. And then reading some more. I had no prior experience working in government, so getting up to speed was essential. Before starting, I had done a lot of studying about the workings of the county but I was still trying to thoroughly understand policies and to get my head around the language that was used in the public sector.

I also began to appreciate the necessity of being able to navigate and manage the politics in local government. County Administrator Darryl Delabbio gave me the book, *Right From the Start*, by Dan Ciampa and Michael D. Watkins. It provided tactical advice about transitioning into a new leadership role of an organization and how to be effective in dealing with the cultural and relational issues. As a member of the executive team, I had to learn the terrain of influencers in the county—who had clout, and how to work with them. Figuring out where the power resided was an important strategy from the beginning.

One thing that I brought with me to the job was an understanding of how to get people to cooperate to solve problems. In line with my mission of serving others, I often thought about how I could be a convener, and how to pull opposing forces together to resolve issues. My experience in sports had prepared me to deal with people from different backgrounds and to get people to work together to get things done. Instead of coming at things from an authoritative mindset, I try to get people to understand what the issues are. Hopefully, through the process, they will stay at the table and collaborate to solve big issues.

My management responsibilities as assistant administrator included the Health Department, liaison with the State Department of Human Services, Kent County Housing and Community Development Department, Senior Services and the Veterans Affairs Department. I was also handed the responsibility for overseeing the county's performance management program, which was still in its infancy and had not yet grown into a system of constructive accountability.

The intent of performance management is to help individuals and teams realize their potential by clearly defining the organization's mission and how each component contributes to overall success. It is a continuous process that enhances communication and provides measurement tools to evaluate, improve and reward performance. Because it encompasses constructive feedback, the process boosts employee engagement and morale, helping an organization reward and retain those workers who exceed expectations.

Of course, you have to know where you're at before you can figure out how to get to where you want to go. During my time at Steelcase I learned the importance of establishing a baseline so we could know where we were starting from and could begin mapping out targets for improvement. As part of the initial process, I went out and interviewed Delabbio and all department heads, elected and appointed, to determine their likes and concerns about the program. Many of them were resisting the new system because it took an unreasonable amount of time to input data and to make good use of it. They believed it did not add value and that the reports would just sit on a shelf. And some feared we were going to try to tell them how to do their jobs.

At Steelcase, we studied the production techniques of Toyota and other companies that adopted lean manufacturing before we put our own world-class manufacturing system in place. Now working for Kent County, I investigated some of the successful performance management systems around the country, including the one implemented by Fairfax County in Virginia. Fairfax was being recognized annually for excellence in performance management by the International City/County Management Association. Fairfax County's performance measures are integrated into its annual budget to ensure accountability and to establish the link between resources and results.

One of the big issues in Kent County was that department heads lacked a system to elicit input and to better understand how they were performing on a regular cadence. You have to be intentional about gathering relevant data, and most departments had no intentionality in this area.

Our reengineering of the performance management system needed to identify and reinforce the fundamental question of why the county and its departments existed and who was the customer. This is true for organizations in both the private and public sectors. For the County of Kent, all citizens of the jurisdiction are its customers. Citizens are critical stakeholders because they pay property taxes and other fees, entrusting their dollars to public officials. That obligates the government to explain what it does and how effectively it is doing it. Being able to clearly communicate this information is an important reason for establishing performance management.

Department heads play an important role in delineating what really matters so that we know what to measure. Equalization Director Matt Woolford, whose department does appraisal studies and tax mapping for the county, recounted how I wanted to know why his department did what it did. And with each answer, I continued to ask "why" as part of the 5 Whys root-cause analysis. In an interview, Matt said:

"What Wayman really wanted to do was coax out of me why we were doing what we were doing. The "why' questions led to the reason my department exists: we're Americans, we have a responsibility to pay taxes but we don't want to pay more than our fair share. With each "why," Wayman peeled away a mindset of outputs and redirected my thoughts towards outcomes. As a result, I was able to communicate a fundamental truth that our department exists to maintain integrity in the property tax system. That resulted in a fundamental shift in our focus. Instead of looking at outputs as the narrative, they became a support for measuring the outcomes, which were the results related to our core function."

Over time, departments learned to use the system as a tool to motivate and inspire excellence among team members. The vast majority of people come to work for reasons beyond just a paycheck. They wonder how they are doing and how they fit in the big equation. They want to know that their work is meaningful, and that it contributes to the success of the overall enterprise. When employees are unsure of where they stand, it can lead to selfish behavior such as blaming, shaming or accusing others. Excuses become the norm. Politics get in the way and no one keeps their eye on the ball.

For those who work in local government, performance management clarifies what is expected and what success in their job looks like. Understanding how they contribute to the overall picture gives people a feeling that they can make a difference. Attaining measurable results affirms that their efforts are valuable and gives them pride of ownership.

We actively solicited input from employees on what they were proud of doing and how we could help them do their jobs better. And to show that their efforts were appreciated, we created an annual Employee Recognition Week to honor and thank employees for their commitment to excellence in service. A letter of appreciation was provided by the county administrator. We also recognized departments who were excellent in achieving community impact, collaboration, innovation and diversity, equity and inclusion through the Excellence in Action program. Winning departments received a letter of appreciation from the chair of the Board of Commissioners and county administrator, they were cited in the county newsletter, and recognized at a board meeting. A special reception was also held with the commissioners and the winners.

We needed to confront a few department heads, including elected officials, who at first resisted implementation of the performance management program. This was done with the utmost diplomacy and tact, of course. The ultimate trump card was the budget, which is proposed by the county administrator and then goes to the Board of Commissioners for approval. Departments knew that if they wanted to add more staffing, or if they wanted to acquire additional funding for capital improvements, their best ammunition was to show how effective and efficient they were at managing their previous budgets.

It was hard to get buy-in from one particular department. They argued that they lacked sufficient staff to do what was expected. We assigned one of our best performance measurements review team members to work with them. The department ended up becoming one of the strongest supporters and advocates for the program.

One of the important components of performance management at Kent County was that department heads were faced every year with the prospect of going in front of the commissioners and the public to tell their story. A side benefit of this was that this helped them to take a critical look at themselves and to then focus on ways of doing better. Department heads learned that implementing performance measurement principles enabled them to effectively communicate their progress. They could point to how much better their teams performed compared to previous years or to how they fared against other counties. Performance management was a mechanism to create an ongoing dialogue about what was needed to be done to improve existing practices and it helped to unearth new ideas for achieving excellence.

Vision, mission, strategy, goals, objectives and indicators all needed to be aligned for our system of performance management to work as it was intended, so we created training components and generated a workbook with procedures that were easy to understand. In short, it provided a pathway for affirming why we existed, for determining what we were going to do about it, plus how were we going to do it. And it provided a consistent way of showing how effective and efficient we were at doing it.

"If we only knew what we know" is a slogan I learned at Steelcase. It reflects the need to develop ways to make sure learnings are shared within different parts of an organization. At Kent County, innovations were cropping up in varying departments at different locations but often weren't being communicated to other segments of the organization. So we brought in an outside data management company, Envisio, to help us corral the information. Their work made it possible for us to develop a huge database that enables best practices to be shared with the Board of Commissioners and all departments. This stored information also provides historical reference for tracking improvements over time.

I am certain that Kent County wasn't the first county in Michigan to implement performance management. But a robust system for tracking, reporting and sharing the performance of all departments of a county, including elected offices and enterprise units like the Public Works Department, had not yet been done. The Michigan Association of Counties featured the practices we put in place, and I believe the Kent County system has grown to be one of the best in the country because of the way we elevated the idea of excellence in everything we do.

CHAPTER 12

The Power of Working Together

I often find that opportunities come disguised as problems. For example, the opening of the beautiful Kent County Human Services Complex in 2009 arose out of an original need to do something about an old, inadequate building that housed the Department of Human Services (DHS). The existing building wasn't a healthy place to conduct business. The lobby was too small to provide comfortable space for people, especially when economic times got tight and more people needed help. Even the elevator didn't work reliably.

For nearly two decades, area leaders had tried unsuccessfully to build an up-to-date facility to house a variety of agencies scattered throughout the county. They had identified buildings and sites. But it was difficult to finalize the project because it involved getting agreement by many constituents. I was asked to take on the task because the DHS was in my domain as assistant administrator.

The first thing we did was determine where most of the clients resided and assess the most available transportation opportunities for them. We mapped by Zip Code the clients that were accessing services, then examined transit patterns for bus, car and proximity to an expressway. When we drew a circle around the location that best fit the needs, it encompassed an area where the county had an existing building near downtown Grand Rapids at 121 Franklin, near Jefferson and Sheldon streets, and only a few blocks west of the former DHS building at 415 Franklin. This proposed new site was the Sheldon Complex, which housed the county's Sheldon Health Clinic that provides immunizations and supplemental nutrition for women, infants and children. Also located there was ACSET West Michigan Works, an agency that meets emergency needs of individuals and families. Michigan Works also evaluates job seekers' strengths and skills and steers them to training opportunities.

The Sheldon Complex was an outdated cinder block building that had seen its best days of use. It had also been a rallying point for community groups to meet, and we wanted to see that this purpose continued. There was some county property behind it, but not enough to accommodate the size and scope needed to bring more services and parking to the site. We would need to acquire additional property to provide a large enough footprint for the staff and visitors to park and conduct business in the building.

Getting all the interested parties to pull together would be the biggest challenge. We met with people who resided in the neighborhood, who worried about traffic and feared their property values would take a hit because of poor people coming to the building. Plus, we needed to acquire property from some of them, as well as from the City of Grand Rapids and the Grand Rapids Public Schools, to make the plan feasible.

Another sensitive issue that came up was the naming of the proposed new facility. The existing DHS building was named in honor of Paul I. Phillip, a trailblazer who had headed the local chapter of the Urban League and was the first Black resident to hold elected office in Grand Rapids. He had been a prominent figure in the African American community during his lifetime. But the new building would house many services and serve a broad swath of the public.

We met with leaders of African American, Latino and Caucasian constituencies and came up with a plan to pay tribute to community leaders of all stripes. We proposed to honor a number of leaders who had led efforts to improve the condition of Kent County residents. This turned out to be a winning solution. We worked with engineers, architects and a graphic artist, eventually coming up with a design for a beautiful 9-foot-tall, 16-foot-long glass exhibit inside the north lobby that showcases 30 people, representing many sectors of the community. And we got everyone to agree that the building would be called the Kent County Human Services Complex.

The size and scope of the project required us to get buy-ins from our DHS Board, the Board of Commissioners, the City of Grand Rapids, the Grand Rapids Public Schools, local state legislators and various community agencies and business leaders. Most of the space would be utilized by State of Michigan agencies, so we also needed to work with the state, which would pay 90 percent of the lease costs. We had to accommodate the state's prescriptive rules for their interior space, number of parking spaces, how the foyer and rest rooms would be placed and other issues. We also needed to negotiate the price they would pay for leasing space. It was not easy dealing with the state bureaucracy but we eventually reached agreement.

After we had reached consensus with the many interested parties, the Kent County Board of Commissioners approved a $27 million bond sale. State lease payment would be applied to paying it off. The plan called for demolishing the old Sheldon building and constructing the new, 133,000-square-foot facility on the site. This meant conducting an environmental study of the location, finding temporary new quarters for the

DHS and ACSET Michigan Works staff, and informing residents of new locations for services.

It took about three years of effort, but the new Human Services Complex opened in the spring of 2009. Residents now can go to one place to find a number of agencies, including the Sheldon Health Clinic, Kent Community Action, ACSET West Michigan Works, DHS Social Services, Children's Protective Services and Adult Protective Services. It is a modern, functional and attractive building in which residents can take pride. And it was the first new building in Kent County to earn LEED (Leadership in Energy and Environmental Design) certification, a recognition bestowed by the U.S. Green Building Council.

From my first days of playing basketball as a youngster in North Carolina, I began learning how teamwork makes a critical difference. As the automotive pioneer Henry Ford once said, "Coming together is a beginning, staying together is progress, and working together is a success." The Kent County Human Services Complex was a prime example of how this kind of cooperative spirit can really improve a community.

Another significant decision we faced during my time as assistant administrator involved deciding whether to support building an addition to the Kent County Correctional Facility. The building dated back to the 1950s, with some expansion in later years.

When the question of enlarging the jail came up, some members of the community pushed back and wanted the county to develop more programs that would provide an alternative to young people ending up in jail. The "pipeline-to-prison" environment was gaining attention throughout the country. Pipeline-to-prison data showed that racial minorities and students with disabilities disproportionately ended up incarcerated for relatively minor and nonviolent violations of the law. We needed to address both issues at the same time, especially because we were going to need voter approval to pay for adding space to the jail. So we simultaneously undertook exhaustive studies.

We did a capacity study on the existing 380,000-square-foot correctional facility, a building that was really showing its age. We met with key leaders in the justice system, including the prosecutor, judges, the sheriff, state probation officials and others. Engineers were brought in to examine the existing facility. The jail system population, both male and female, had been growing and reached more than 30,000 a year by 2010, with inmates staying for an average of 15 days.

The existing facility consisted of 430 linear maximum-custody beds, a 48-bed dormitory, and 56 additional beds that had been added in the 1970s. Grand Rapids-based architectural firm TowerPinkster worked with design firm HOK to develop several potential layouts. One issue that arose was that the mechanical and electrical structure in the oldest part of the building had badly deteriorated.

We eventually chose a proposal that included demolishing the oldest parts of the original jail, renovating the additions that had been subsequently made, and adding a new three-story pod consisting of 85,000 square feet and 320 beds. The plan was to complete the project in phases in order to allow the jail to continue to operate during construction. The layout improved direct supervision capability, a concept that has been found to reduce violence in cells and improve safety for supervising staff. The design also allowed for better locations for the kitchen, laundry, and the jail health clinic. It was also designed to enable future expansion, if needed.

The proposal drew resistance from four cities within the county that had shut down their own jails in order to house their prisoners in the county facility. They demanded that we stop charging them a per-diem fee for those inmates if there was going to be a new millage. We eventually settled this problem by renegotiating the per diem rate.

Then we found out something interesting through our Alternatives to Incarceration study. It turned out that some judges had a much greater propensity to sentence people to jail rather than choosing alternative sentences such as work release, community service, probation, deferred sentences and other options. In order to encourage judges to rethink who should end up being held in jail, Sheriff Larry Stelma worked out a plan to allocate a certain number of beds for each judge based on the number of cases that came before them.

The Alternatives to Incarceration report was filed with the Board of Commissioners. The report educated the community on the numerous methods and programs that were underway to stave off the need to house people in jail. Kent County was on the leading edge of this thinking. It became a non-issue in the campaign to get voters to approve a millage proposal to pay for the $27 million expansion and upgrade. Voters okayed the ballot issue and the project was completed in 2012.

It was Peter Secchia's idea to bring the Big 10 Women's Basketball Tournament to Van Andel Arena in 2001 as a way to stimulate the local economy. Despite $250,000 spent to support the event, attendance was a bust. But the lessons learned kick-started a movement that brought the community together to establish the West Michigan Sports Commission

(WMSC) in 2007. The commission has helped make West Michigan a destination for amateur youth and adult sports activities. Through its first 13 years, the WMSC booked 882 events, attracted more than 1.4 million athletes and generated over $410 million in direct visitor spending.

Peter was a successful businessman, a confidante of the 38th U.S. President Gerald R. Ford, and served as ambassador to Italy during his career. He was also a philanthropist who made major donations to Michigan State University. This generosity included $5 million he and his wife Joan donated to help establish MSU's Grand Rapids Research Center, which is dedicated to improving human health.

After the setback with the Big 10 women's tournament, Peter came to the Kent County Board of Commissioners to ask for assistance in establishing a sports commission to help market the area as an attractive destination for athletic events. He pointed to Minneapolis, St. Louis, Orlando and other cities whose commissions were bringing in sports tourist dollars. He challenged the board to get on board with funding support instead of leaving it completely to the private sector.

The commissioners were interested because the county's hotel/motel tax proceeds were earmarked to pay off bonds for DeVos Place, the convention center located in downtown Grand Rapids. When the hotel/motel tax didn't produce enough money, the county (and its taxpayers) had to pick up the rest of the tab. During economic downturns, the county has been left holding the bag for as much as $7 million out of its general funds to make bond payments. There were a number of beautiful hotels in the Grand Rapids area, but their occupancy rates ebbed and flowed. We needed to create more reasons for visitors to come into town on a regular basis.

The county did two studies, one of them led by my team. While the other study recommended against getting involved with a sports commission, my team conducted research around the country, and the information collected revealed that amateur sports was a $16 billion industry in the United States. We reported back on the things we needed to do to make it work and advised that we should go for it.

One of the keys to making the sports commission successful was to set it up as a nonprofit agency with 501(c)(3) status. None of its earnings would go to a private shareholder or individual and the nonprofit status appealed to people across the area. Because the sports commission would be standing on its own, it wouldn't be perceived as a quasi-government entity. It would get some funding from Kent County, but it could also attract support from the Grand Rapids/Kent County Convention and Visitors Bureau (Experience Grand Rapids), the Grand Rapids/Kent County Convention Arena Authority and from the private sector.

The Board of Commissioners approved the concept and we established the West Michigan Sports Commission (WMSC) in 2007, with its mission to attract and host youth and amateur sporting events to enhance the region's economy and quality of life. And it soon got a big boost from Floyd Mayweather, the great boxing champion who was born in Grand Rapids. Mayweather first got noticed when he won the Michigan Golden Gloves competition. He then went on to win 15 major world championships in five weight classes before retiring undefeated in 50 fights.

Just as the WMSC was gearing up, Floyd was looking for ways to give something back to the region where he grew up. He and his manager, Leonard Ellerbe, formed Mayweather Promotions and they agreed to work with us to bring the 2008 national Golden Gloves Tournament of Champions to DeVos Place in Grand Rapids. Mayweather Promotions presented us a check for $140,000, the entire operating budget for the tournament, for the WMSC. The donation also made it possible to give free tickets to area underprivileged kids to attend the three-day event.

From the beginning, the WMSC held successful annual luncheons with guest speakers to raise funds. Tickets go fast. The first year, I used my University of Michigan connections to help bring in John Beilein, the Wolverines head basketball coach. The next year, Peter Secchia leveraged his Michigan State network to bring in renowned MSU basketball coach Tom Izzo. One year, Peter and I combined to help get Michigan Football Coach Lloyd Carr and former MSU Football Coach George Perles on the same stage for the luncheon.

Meijer Inc., a chain of Midwest supercenters, is one of the private sector companies that has supported WMSC activities from the beginning. Meijer headquarters are in Walker, which is part of the Grand Rapids metropolitan area. Kent County donated property and the Road Commission helped to provide some of the infrastructure for the championship-caliber sports complex, owned and operated by the WMSC in Rockford. The main title sponsor for the complex was originally the furniture company Art Van Furniture, but Meijer eventually took over the prime sponsorship.

There are nine baseball/softball fields now at the Meijer Sports Complex for local youth leagues as well as statewide, regional and national tournaments for youth and adult teams. One of the nine is Miracle Field, which is dedicated for use by athletes who face physical or mental disabilities. In 2021, the complex welcomed 25 tournaments and 684 teams. The nearly 9,000 athletes and 22,000 spectators booked about 6,000 hotel room nights bringing in an estimated $5.6 million.

The Meijer State Games are also big draws. Held throughout the West Michigan area, the Games involve dozens of summer and winter Olympic-style events for amateurs of all ages and abilities. Like the Olympics, the Meijer State Games include Opening Ceremonies, a Parade of Athletes and Lighting of the Cauldron. The WMSC is also involved with activities such as the annual Metro Health Grand Rapids Marathon, the Amway River Bank Run and the Jr. Wheelchair Basketball Tournament.

The WSMC has generated economic benefits for the area and has boosted the image of West Michigan. It has also brought people together around the idea of enriching the lives of young people through participation in sports. I absorbed a lot about the importance of working together and becoming a leader during my years of playing organized basketball. Seeing today's youth competing and growing their character and leadership ability through sports gives me great hope and satisfaction that the quality of life and future of our community will be brighter.

CHAPTER 13

Empowering Others

I have learned that the role of government should be to empower people. Power is a funny thing—the more you give, the more you get. People want to know that you care about their goals and aspirations before they care about yours. Too often in government, we get this backwards. Our role in government includes keeping order, protecting rights and ensuring justice is served. But in so doing, we must guard against our tendency to over-control and thus limit the ability of our community partners to contribute solutions for our issues.

When Kent County Administrator Daryl Delabbio retired, the Board of Commissioners appointed me on July 1, 2017 as interim administrator. Technically, there was an assistant administrator, Mary Swanson, who had been with the county longer than me. Daryl had considered Mary as his number one assistant. Mary brought a lot to the table, but I had never held back from contributing my talents and connections to the county. The board tapped me for the job while it began a national search for Delabbio's official replacement.

I wasn't sure if I should throw my hat into the ring for the position because the role had become increasingly more political. A few board members didn't want me to have the job. I knew that some favored bringing in someone new to the county with no affiliation with the current administration. I also learned that some on the board wanted someone who thought and looked more like them. But my friend and former University of Michigan basketball teammate Campy Russell told me I had an obligation to show local young people that an African American could rise to this level. No African American had held the position before, and I knew in my heart that Campy was right.

About 70 people applied for the position, and the commissioners eventually narrowed down the field to me and one candidate from the East Coast who had an impressive background in finance. But he dropped out when he saw that he wouldn't have the same level of community support that I had. On January 24, 2018, the Board of Commissioners promoted me to the role of administrator/controller.

I believe it's important for local governments to act transparently, communicate effectively about their services and actions, and solicit input from all members of the community. Marginalized members of the community are too often left out of conversations that affect their lives. Broad community engagement brings diverse perspective and ideas to the table. In the end, citizens feel more like they own decisions, even if they don't agree with every detail. This is the essence of democracy.

One of the first things I did as administrator was to work with my executive team to align our strategy with the most important actions to propel us forward. We developed six strategies that guided our efforts.

INCREASE INNOVATION—Continuously improve the performance and capabilities of county operations by maximizing the use of technology, fostering innovation, and increasing access to information regarding services. Addressing the County's technology deficit will enhance the delivery of county government services by ensuring availability, integrity and security of vital data.

ESTABLISH A SHARED CONSCIOUSNESS—By creating a unified vision and working toward common goals, a unified leadership team will encourage trust, create empowerment, and break managers out of the "my department" mentality and into the "our organization" mentality. Once the admin team has agreed to the overarching unified vision of county administration, it is important that the team determines underlying root problems that may be causing the ripple effect of silos.

RAISE KENT COUNTY'S PROFILE—Step out of the shadow of others and counter efforts that have sought to define or limit the county and its impact on community quality of life. Proactively share the county's successes and how they have increased efficiency, resulting in new collaborations and partnerships, and added value to taxpayers. Work to position the county to become a sought-after partner and community influencer. Reverse the tendency to be reticent about accomplishments.

LEVERAGE DATA AND DATA ANALYTICS—Address important local issues by exploring and downloading relevant open data, analyzing and combining the datasets using maps, and discovering and building apps. Utilize datasets in several formats to create reports of critical information that can be used to shape and inform policy. Ensure a more robust use of available tools, like GIS mapping, for planning and to increase specificity in addressing gaps in service.

GROW TALENT/PEOPLE—Only by engaging the contributions and untapped potential of its workforce can Kent County succeed in the pursuit of excellence. The skills and talents of the

Kent County workforce impacts the success for the community. Establish an expectation that everyone can learn, grow and develop. Be intentional about helping people grow to realize their potential. Devise pathways to help people become engaged and to be more willing and open to sharing their ideas. Work with HR to equip leaders with the tools and skills needed to address difficult situations and people issues. Utilize methods such as Gallup surveys to gauge employee engagement. Improve organizational/departmental culture to help drive results. Teach leaders how to effectively and constructively confront bad behavior.

INCREASE INTERNAL COMMUNICATIONS—Improve/redevelop our intranet as a communication tool to allow for more timely dissemination of information. Expand the distribution of the weekly administrator's report and send out relevant, timely information about what we do. Conduct more regular all-employee communications, highlighting information being shared with the board. Encourage department heads to tell the success stories of their employees. Employ a communications professional that will ensure a consistent delivery method and deal with the multiple Kent County Facebook pages, Twitter accounts, etc., and develop a style guide and communications standard that ensures the consistency of the county's brand.

Effective and robust communications is vital for the well-being of employees and healthy team environments within county administration, and it was important for the overall performance of the county. An informed and engaged workforce produces better results across all levels and all county departments. My team developed print, internet and social media methods to make sure people understood the services available to them. We encouraged departments to get the word out about what county government does, why it does it, and how citizens can provide input. For example, several videos were made around Friend of the Court issues such as parenting time, child support and mediation. We educated people about the judicial system, what to do if they get behind on taxes, and how to make sure they knew what they needed to do if they were running a business. In addition to helping people take advantage of resources, this information also stirred more citizen interest in joining committees in order to improve things.

To help people take advantage of resources, we improved our web site—www.accesskent—where they can find information about important issues facing the community, information on boards and committees of the county, as well as livestream meetings. The site breaks down programs and services so that residents know what they do. And if someone is interested in joining a commission or running for a board position, the information is all there. We wanted all citizens to know what they could do to have influence on what we did.

In another move to heighten transparency, in 2019 we conducted the county's first joint public State of the County address. I focused on the role of the county as a regional and state convener in dealing with perplexing issues, highlighting the initiatives underway and the progress the county had made. Board of Commissioners Chair Mandy Bolter delivered remarks about efforts to improve the quality of life of the region.

We also worked with the Board of Commissioners to develop a Kent County Strategic Plan for the five-year period starting in 2019. During the process, we gathered input from county residents, elected officials including all county commissioners, judicial officials, and county partners in the phil-anthropic and business community. The plan established five priorities aligned with the county's values, vision and mission. The priorities are economic prosperity, high quality of life, excellence in service delivery, inclusive participation and effective communications. We set specific goals to achieve within each priority.

I saw county government as a vehicle for helping to create prosperity for every resident. We were not just in the policing business, the justice business, or the public works and trash-collecting business. My belief was that our ultimate goal was to leverage and manage our resources to the fullest extent possible so that our community thrives, and that each person has the opportunity to reach their full potential. The challenge was to figure out how to create a flourishing and prosperous community for all who would come after us.

Finding common ground to bring people together is essential to achieving this ideal. And having the ability to rally the community to get things done hinged upon how successful we were in establishing and nurturing key relationships. An example of this is how we began tackling the mental health issue in Kent County.

Among the most vulnerable people in any community are those with mental health issues. Far too often, they end up in jails or hospital emergency rooms instead of a place where they can get appropriate help. We approached this issue from an integrated system perspective that would require both government and private-area participation. The county took on an active role in coordinating the planning process for a mental health crisis center to provide care any time of day for people, regardless of their insurance coverage. But the county would not own and operate the system.

We established the Kent County Population Health Consortium, a group that included mental health agencies, heads of hospitals and others in the medical field, including people like Mike Jandernoa, former chairman and CEO of Perrigo Co., a West Michigan-based healthcare supplier of generic prescription pharmaceuticals and other medications. Mike has served on boards of directors for hospital and other medical-related boards, and his stature in the community helped to get CEOs on board. Mike also was campaign chair for the local Heart of West Michigan United Way and pulled me into their fundraising efforts, and I in turn sought his input on issues where he had expertise. My goal as administrator was to find people like this because it takes experts in both the public and private sectors to solve some of the complex problems we faced.

In 2019 we hired consultancy Tri-West to come up with a plan for the crisis system and how to pay for it. Area hospitals paid about 75% of the $321,000 cost with the county chipping in the rest. By early 2021 the plan evolved to possibly include mobile crisis response units, a call center and two crisis campuses. The county awarded a $255,000 contract to TBD Solutions, a consultancy in nearby Kentwood, to complete the planning work by year's end. About $85,000 of the contract was to come from private and public healthcare partners who had a stake in the plan. When I left office in July 2021, I was confident we were on the right track to providing timely, professional care to residents in mental health crisis.

A fundamental role for every government is thoughtful budgeting and planning to ensure a high quality of life for its residents. The Great Recession, which began in late 2007 and lasted until mid-2009, dramatically hampered county and municipal governments. The collapse of the housing market reduced property tax revenues while the flow of state and federal aid was cut back because of lower income tax and sales tax proceeds.

Like many other local entities, Kent County put off needed capital improvement projects. We prepared a proposal to move forward with three projects that had been stalled. We brought in Progressive A&E, a Grand Rapids architecture and engineering firm, to develop plans and an eye-opening presentation for the Board of Commissioners. We were able to convey the importance of moving these projects forward, and the board approved $18.7 million for the three projects.

About two-thirds of the money was budgeted to create a campus in the northern tier of the county in Cedar Springs to establish a hub that would better serve residents. This part of the county is less densely populated than the southern section that included Grand Rapids. The new building would consolidate a Health Department clinic and Sheriff's Office substation. Groundbreaking took place in October 2021 for the 30,000-square-foot office space, which could be used for some additional services such as Kent County Community Action, Veteran Services and the Friend of the Court.

Another $2.67 million was approved for a permanent Kent County Parks Department building near Millennium Park, replacing a trailer facility. Millennium Park is one of the country's largest urban parks. It's a real gem, with rolling terrain in four cities along the Grand River and a combination of natural areas, playgrounds and recreational opportunities such as swimming, fishing and boating.

The final piece of the capital improvements was $3.5 million to expand our vehicle repair and maintenance facility in Grand Rapids. By the time this project was approved, the facility was servicing nearly 300 vehicles, compared with 35 vehicles when it was placed into service in 1957.

Another issue Kent County needed to address for the future was agricultural preservation. Grand Rapids is a midsize American city, but much of the territory outside of its immediate area consists of farmland. Apples, other crops, livestock and poultry are all part of a farming scene that makes a significant economic contribution and provides fresh food supply. We did not want to see haphazard urban sprawl push farms out of existence, which has happened in many other regions.

Kent County is one of the fastest growing areas in Michigan, resulting in development pressure on farmland. It's really the responsibility of various townships to manage planning and zoning which dovetails into the farmland property rights issue, but advocates were coming to the county asking it to fund the purchase of farm property for agriculture preservation. But the county had limited resources and could only provide a small fraction of the funding that was needed for the purchase of farmland that had been identified for preservation in the county. It was not enough to be able to say we had actually achieved what we set out to do.

My team articulated a convincing argument to the Board of Commissioners that the current approach was not working. While the townships were the planning jurisdiction, the county needed to be part of the discussion to ensure we do things in a collective and thoughtful manner, including planning for infrastructure improvements where they would be needed. And instead of buying farmland, we began discussing a program called "transfer of development rights," a voluntary program which pays owners of farmland for their willingness to accept a deed restriction on their land to limit the future development for non-agricultural purposes. Although we were just in the beginning stages of the discussion with the board, many were beginning to see this as a win for the townships, the farmers, and the county.

CHAPTER 14

Managing Crisis

"Everybody has a plan until they get punched in the mouth."
– MIKE TYSON

C hampion boxer Mike Tyson gave this blunt answer when a reporter asked him about strategy for an upcoming fight. It is a truism that applies to many aspects of life. Our ability to respond to unexpected adversity is a big part of determining success.

When a crisis affects a country or a community, people look to government to help identify this issue and direct action. During my time as administrator, Kent County needed to react locally to some challenges that affected the entire country. One of those issues arose after a controversial decision was made by the federal government to step up enforcement actions by the U.S. Immigration and Customs Enforcement (ICE).

Like many other jurisdictions, Kent County had previously worked out a cooperative agreement with ICE to hold immigrant detainees for ICE without a judicial warrant. For years, ICE had only focused on undocumented immigrants who had committed serious crimes. The effects of the new hardline stance landed in our laps. The controversy escalated in our community in December 2018 when Jilmar Ramos-Gomez, a 27-year-old Marine veteran, was arrested and held in the Kent County Jail on charges related to trespassing and damaging a fire alarm in a hospital. Ramos-Gomez, a U.S. citizen who was born and raised in Michigan, suffered from post-traumatic syndrome after his service in Afghanistan. He was handed over to ICE upon the agency's request. This set off protest demonstrations about racial profiling and raised fear and anxiety in the Latino community. Ramos-Gomez was eventually released by ICE after three days of confinement.

We took the same approach to this concern that we established for other issues—research, talk to the community, and formulate a win-win answer if possible. We worked with the City of Grand Rapids, the Community Foundation, Grand Rapids Chamber of Commerce, Hispanic community leaders and others so that we could find a solution that put the county in the driving role. Our goal was to protect the safety of the community while also calming the worries of immigrants. We wanted a Kent County answer rather than something imposed on us.

Sheriff Michelle LaJoye-Young put one part of our response in place when she announced her department would no longer hold immigrant detainees for ICE without an arrest warrant signed by a federal judge. This brought due process into the equation to protect citizens like Ramos-Gomez. Eventually, ICE chose to cancel its jail contract with Kent County.

At the same time, Lori Latham, our communications and government relations director, took the lead in formulating a plan to make immigrants feel more secure and welcome. A multi-sector partnership called Gateways for Growth was organized to focus on creating a more hospitable environment for new Americans in Kent County. The steering committee included individuals from Kent County, the City of Grand Rapids, West Michigan Hispanic Chamber of Commerce, Grand Rapids Chamber of Commerce and the nonprofit social services agency Samaritas. The group worked with a task force of 36 community organizations.

The committee found that immigrants and refugees were a growing part of the area's population and played key roles in the workforce of agriculture, manufacturing and hospitality. The group developed a set of goals to promote welcoming immigrants and help them integrate into the community. The recommendations to create this kind of hospitable atmosphere focused on civic engagement, economic development, safe and connected communities, education, and equitable access to services.

I am a strong believer that diversity is an under-tapped resource and strength for our society. Men and women with different backgrounds contribute distinct experiences and perspectives to solving problems. But the death of George Floyd, pinned to the ground by a police officer's knee in Minneapolis, underscored the racial divide that still exists in America. Demonstrations erupted across the country, and in some cities—including Grand Rapids—protests were marred by clashes with police and destructive actions that damaged both public and private property.

It was important to find a way to address concerns about systemic racism while also acknowledging that our law enforcement officers have a necessary but difficult job to do in protecting life and property. I conveyed my thoughts in a virtual meeting with county departments. These are some of my remarks:

> *The fear and outrage that has gripped us, the anger that has gripped us, has affected every sector of our community. We believe now is the time to listen and to hear from you and to be able to talk about how we are going to deal with the aftermath of something we know should have never happened. We are not alone in this. There are others in this community who truly*

care about what has happened. We're going to work together to do some things that will fix it.

I talked with the Board of Commissioners, our chair, about this meeting today to make sure we elevate the discussion about systemic racism—the fact that we still have not arrived at a place where every human being in our country is treated as an equal, valued member of society to the extent that they can have a full life...

Not every officer behaves that way. Our Sheriff's Department, the people who wear our uniform, from my 16 years working with the county and interacting with the Sheriff's Department, I can tell you that these outstanding officers are here to protect our community. The moral standard, the respect they have for our community should be an example of how all departments should interact with our community. Police reform is needed. I can tell you the City of Grand Rapids is working on that. We have a meeting with the City of Grand Rapids, we are interested in what we can do working alongside of them.

I know that Sheriff Michelle Young's staff stands by her in what she's attempting to do to make sure the culture that we all believe in, the culture that believes in treating others with respect and dignity, and valuing another person's life, is really the hallmark of how all of you feel about how we should interact with our community. I am a firm believer that if we do that together, we can change the world. The example we set is critical. How we manage and support one another is critical...

I never thought that at this time in history we would see a situation where the community was in an uproar, where there were riots happening on our streets, and that people were protesting to the point where they were damaging our buildings. It's with heavy heart that I come today with you seeking a way out of this, trying to figure out what can we do as an orga-nization and as a community to live out our values and to figure out how we set the example for how we live together, how we work together and how we change the way that our society behaves. And it will take all of us.

You've asked what can you do? How can you help? This webinar is the starting point for that. We don't have the answers. But you have insights, you have ideas that can help us. We are going to ask every department and every employee to give input on this call today. And we're going to stay united. This is not a sprint. This is not a marathon. It is more like a 440-hurdle relay whereby we will need to work together. How do we pass the baton to the Sheriff's Office, to our Circuit Court, to our Veteran Service Department, our District Court, our Public Works Department, Drain Com-missioner, Prosecutor, Clerk's Office, Health Department? How do we join together and take advantage of the oppor-tunity to build a better place? We are doing a lot of good things but we need to do more. We have to get real about the reality that some of us are not there yet. Sometimes it's not intentional. Sometimes it's the way life comes at us, we react with anger that doesn't help, it hurts. We have to un-derstand that. I just hope and pray that it never comes back that we didn't do anything, that we sat idle, that we didn't challenge ourselves. I hope and pray that it comes back that we were willing to look at ourselves and ask, "What can I do to make sure this never happens again?"

We then had a panel discussion led by several department heads, who also fielded questions from employees. It's not easy to have productive conversations about race equity. Even well-intentioned people may feel uncomfortable or fear they will be judged.

But these discussions are overdue. We must learn to listen to each other in order to create a culture where everyone is treated with respect and dignity. Honest conversations are an essential step in resolving misperceptions, understanding each other and grasping how racial barriers affect all of our lives.

In 2009, US Airways pilot Chester "Sully" Sullenberger skillfully executed an emergency landing in the Hudson River near midtown Manhattan, saving all 155 people on board. Sully later said he had to pull together everything he had ever learned to successfully resolve the crisis.

In March 2020, the Covid pandemic became a national emergency in the United States. I needed to pull together all I had learned to help Kent County steer through this unexpected crisis. Local governments were on the front lines in trying to maintain crucial services during a time when much of the private sector was on shutdown.

I learned to be adaptable through experiencing other emergency situations such as recessions, but this time was different. Lives were at stake, not just budgets. It was a massive job. Fortunately, my tremendously talented team, Kent County elected officials, and other partners in the community all brought their "A game" to the dire situation. It was a testament to the quality of people in Kent County.

We constantly adjusted operations in response to the latest information and community need. We quickly mobilized the county Health Department to establish Covid testing sites, conduct contact tracing and develop various communication pieces to ensure our community response was timely, efficient, and equitable. The West Michigan Vaccine Clinic at DeVos Place in downtown Grand Rapids administered as many as 12,000 shots a day. And we secured two vehicles to facilitate community-based health services to distribute Covid-19 vaccines to residents who could not easily access other vaccination sites. We worked closely with other health care partners, schools and universities, faith leaders, and businesses throughout the pandemic to ensure access to resources to prevent illness and death.

In the early months of the pandemic, our tracing revealed disparities in rates of infection among ethnic groups, with African Americans, Latinos and people who identified as Asian all having higher rates. To address this situation, the Health Department and its Race, Equity and Inclusion Team met regularly with community groups that represent these constituencies. This gave them a voice in selecting community testing sites, developing and sharing educational materials, conducting contact tracing and ensuring equitable access to other resources. These efforts substantially reduced the disparities. I believe our response overall was a major reason Kent County's Covid mortality rate in 2020 was less than half of Michigan's overall rate.

The biggest issue that kept me up at night was making sure we were ready during constantly evolving conditions. Early on, we held meetings every day to get feedback from all departments and ensured that they had the right resources to respond to the situation at hand. Every Friday we met virtually with all the local units of government to share information and ideas. Meeting with community groups, we identified hot spots and opened coronavirus isolation centers for homeless people in order to reduce spread of the illness and to keep hospital beds available for those with more severe needs. And in collaboration with Michigan State University College of Human Medicine, Spectrum Health, Mercy Health Saint Mary's and major businesses such as Meijer,

Steelcase, Amway and the City of Grand Rapids we developed guidelines and best practices for businesses planning to reopen. We cooperated with judges to enable them to conduct court sessions virtually as much as possible. Additionally, we designed and implemented a formal Covid Preparedness and Response Plan to provide county employees with critical and relevant employer-based health, safety, and occupational policy information.

Having many of our employees working remotely was uncharted territory. We were successful in implementing a large-scale remote work plan, including the deployment of several hundred new laptop computers for the transition to a primarily remote-capable work force. We needed to implement changes to the traditional IT service model to maximize security and workflow as well as make it possible to use county phone services from remote locations.

Like other local governments throughout the country, our revenues took a big hit even as the pandemic required us to increase spending in critical areas. We were one of four counties in Michigan to receive a direct CARES (Coronavirus Aid, Relief, and Economic Security) allocation from the U.S. Department of Treasury. We worked with a subcommittee of the Board of Commissioners to establish an inclusive process to allocate the $114.6 million of federal money. Groups such as United Way and the Grand Rapids Chamber of Commerce met with us to assess ways we could best help the community. Our primary goals were to slow the spread of the virus and to assist those facing financial hardship.

The Board of Commissioners eventually allocated $34 million to the Small Business Relief Program, providing grants to 3,545 local businesses. About $33 million was directed to county expenses related to the pandemic and nearly $15 million went to local units of government.

Nonprofit organizations received more than $9 million in grants and another $8 million-plus went to mitigate homelessness and help community residents stay in their homes. School districts received about $3 million to help them safely reopen. In addition, money was allocated to add wi-fi hotspots, provide personal protective equipment to small employers, and give aid for the John Ball Zoo and the Convention Arena Authority.

These are just a few highlights of our overall response to the pandemic. I am most proud of the way so many elements of the community worked together. The county couldn't do it on its own. We led on some issues, and stepped aside when others were in the best position to do so. The response to the Covid crisis is a powerful example of how communities can achieve great things by working together and empowering others.

Leading Change

When you're blamed and shamed for something, how do you feel? Let's say I call you up one day and I tell you how bad you are and how you should've done it this way, should've done it that way, and you did this wrong and did that wrong. How do you feel about me when I do that to you? Do you want me to call you back? Do you want to have a conversation again with me anytime soon? Do you want to listen to me?

Political divisions run deep in the United States. Solutions are hard to negotiate when partisans demonize each other, and leaders play the game of firing up their own base instead of talking with each other. We've got to find a different way. Before we point the finger, we ought to ask ourselves, will the pointing help people swallow and digest the change we want? Will the finger pointing create ownership of the problem and will it help to fix it? Will it prompt the change we want? Often, it just bounces off and nothing ever changes. Whether Democrat or Republican, Black or White, we must talk to each other and listen to each other more.

We need to learn how to pause and reflect on both sides of the situation by considering the opposite. Change often falters in part because those wanting to make the change have a single point of view, which they believe is the whole and perfect solution. Two opposing points of view create tension, yet both are needed in order for the best solution to surface. The other side, and those closer to it, have their own view and regardless of a final agreement both will always exist. You cannot have one without the other so, to some degree, you must embrace the opposite to find a way to move forward.

In order to make positive change happen, we must regain trust. Trust is the currency of democracy and the working capital of innovative governments. To regain trust, we must first understand that unity does not mean homogeny. We will always have differences, particularly the further we go from our own front door.

If you don't advocate for change, people will typically just continue to do what they've been doing. Keeping the status quo is the more comfortable and easier thing to do, but in the long run it's not the right thing to do. Understanding this reality led me to think about how I might best take responsibility in my role with the county to impact the troubling issues facing our community. And I learned if you don't listen, and appreciate what others bring to the table, you won't earn the trust and commitment to contribute to the change you want to make.

By 2045, people of color are projected to make up more that 50% of the US population. And by one estimate, it will take 330 years of advancement at the current rate for minority businesses enterprises in our country to achieve revenue parity. For future generations to thrive, there needs to be a greater commitment to assist more Black businesses in reaching revenue parity. We need to change the narrative about Black families struggling to gain a greater share of the economic pie.

Going back to my days as captain of the state champion

Flint Northern High School basketball team, I had to figure out how to get along with my fellow teammates and how to work together in order to win championships. I didn't shy away from this responsibility. Likewise, in my leadership role at Kent County, I did not hesitate to develop relationships with people of all ethnicities and political stripes in order to build a better community. Just like in the altercation with a fellow teammate and rising star on the Flint Northern team, rather than casting stones, I looked at what we were doing or not doing and appreciated what others brought to the table in order to advance our goals.

In 2016, when I still was assistant administrator, several other Black business leaders and I were working with the Grand Rapids Community Foundation to figure out how to grow more sizable minority businesses. I raised the idea of bringing others to the table like Mike Jandernoa, co-founder of investment banking firm 42 North, former CEO of pharmaceutical company Perrigo and co-founder of Jandernoa Entrepreneurial Mentoring. Then someone asked why we should bring in "an old White guy" like Mike who would tell the group what to do. The fear was that working with Mike would put the group in "the back pocket" of the White power structure in the area.

I was offended. Did they think I wasn't smart enough to recognize if someone was intent on making us their puppet? Mike had created a mentorship program for small businesses of a certain size, and I believed we should capitalize on his knowledge and insight. Unfortunately, it was determined that it wasn't a good idea at all, and the proposal fizzled out.

Interestingly enough, a very short time later I had breakfast with Frank Stanek, newly appointed CEO of construction company Owen-Ames-Kimball. One of the first things he shared with me was his excitement about being involved with

10 other CEOs in the mentoring program established by Mike Jandernoa. Hearing his excitement about being involved with 10 other CEOs in the mentoring program established by Mike made me even more committed and confident about involving individuals like him to help grow more minority-owned businesses and tackle other social problems.

The reality is the Black community doesn't have the wealth to fund all the initiatives that are needed to help lift us up and to create economic parity. Where do you go to get help? You go to where the wealth and the heart are to gain the resources that are needed. If I had shared the negative attitude towards Mike, we never would have been able to put together a strong consortium—made up of hospitals, other health specialists, business executives and government—that developed plans to address the mental health crisis in the area. Sometimes we fail to see the value that others can bring to the table to help solve problems.

We can truly change the game in our society and make it equitable for everyone, but it requires our looking at the entire ecosystem—political, social and economic—and our coming to grip with the disparities that exist in health outcomes, median household income, people in poverty, home ownership, family net worth, unemployment and incarceration rates. It will take caring people working together with a shared vision for future generations to thrive and to overcome these inequalities.

The systems that are at play are powerfully designed and constructed to get the results that that we have been getting. Policy construct dictates who gets to rise and who gets to stand still, or not rise at all. Systemic change will require leaders who are willing to seek out and initiate the change that's needed rather than waiting for someone else to make it happen.

It is all about the mindset. I am an optimistic person by nature—the glass is always half full, not half empty. If we believe that we can solve problems, we can and we will. The question I must ask myself is, how can I contribute to the solutions? And how must I grow my ability to confront issues, help people understand, and grow our collective ability to make positive change?

Racism is both overt and covert, and in some cases, it is based more on a lack of understanding and knowledge than on malice. I think it is a misstep to call it out as something so egregious to the point that it would alienate someone I want to listen to me. To chain them to the idea that their greed or their racism is the sole reason for our social problems just makes them defensive. Sometimes we ignore the reality that there are things we do, that I do, that might hamper our ability to design a better way. Being right about an issue is meaningless unless we can be effective in changing it.

People like Mike can help speed the process of change, and help the minority community grow to economic parity. In Mike's case, he helped build a multi-billion-dollar company, and knew how to get things done—so why shouldn't we leverage his business savvy and experience? My goal as administrator of Kent County was to build relationships with people like him. I figured it was going to take the private and public sector working together to right the inequities that existed and to help move the county forward. I wanted to develop relationships with them, work with them and ultimately get them to help solve some of the pressing issues that existed in the community.

Sometimes people in the business community will use their influence to have strategic advantage over other voices. My sense was that Mike wasn't like that. He was sensitive to the needs of the many and he valued my knowledge and experience. I didn't believe he would undermine my role and drown my influence.

How do we get more people to see the value of sharing power and advantage? How do we get them to truly understand the benefit of relinquishing some of it? They need to understand that holding onto all the power and wealth hurts themselves, their children, their grandchildren and the community in the long run. When inequalities are ignored, it inevitably wastes human potential, fosters more social problems and costs more taxpayer dollars.

I did my best to put the community's needs above my own and tried to get others to see the value of this attitude. This was essentially what I did when I played basketball. I learned to sacrifice for the good of the team. Here are key lessons I've learned about teamwork:

The more I helped my teammates, the more they helped me become a better team member.

The more I thought about how my efforts contributed to the team, the more connected I felt to the overall mission, the intended goal, the driving purpose.

The more committed I was to the driving purpose of the team, the more my individual performance improved.

My wife Dinah reminded me of the power of the team in a story about the flight of geese. Whenever you see geese flying in the V-formation, they are traveling with a greater sense of purpose and direction. They fly together, each taking turns at the head position so they don't get too exhausted from the wind resistance. When one gets tired, another takes over. They honk to encourage one another. Scientists say that flying in that V-formation helps them soar 71 percent more efficiently. Geese are the epitome of strong teamwork that makes it possible to achieve incredible things.

Like geese flying in the V-formation, that sense of working together was the key to ultimately fulfilling our mission to improve the quality of life for the citizens we served in Kent

County. I was often called "coach" because I brought with me a lot of what I learned from my days on the basketball court and winning championships. Great teams trust each other and they expect nothing but the best out of each other. They help each other to succeed.

In mentoring, there is great value for the mentee and the mentor because the relationship creates growth and awareness for each person. I would not have become the leader I am today without people who mentored me along the way. In every organization, it is critical that leaders take seriously the development of the next generation of leaders. I was always conscious of this and the importance of making time to coach and mentor my direct reports and pushing them to be coaches for their staffs. We conducted leadership conferences, training sessions, one-on-one meetings and regular team meetings to make sure we were on the same page and that they had everything they needed to be effective.

When I retired from my position as administrator for Kent County in July 2021, I left believing we had built one of the best teams in America. The people who remained working for the county understood how to get things done. My hope was that others would say that I was an inspiration and helped them attain all they were meant to become.

So it gave me great joy to get feedback I received from one of my staff members who thanked me for helping them grow personally and professionally. This person wrote that my leadership was built from a framework of empowerment and advocacy and that I helped them to face county-wide challenges with the confidence to engage from their strengths, and to overcome their limitations. Moreover, I was delighted by the comment that I made them feel that their voice counted, that I didn't dismiss their views, and that what they had to say mattered.

Another person who had worked for the county posted on a web site that he had started using "Waymanisms" that he picked up from me. Matthew VanZetten, who served as my assistant administrator and management analyst, wrote:

For my children: "Be a leader, not a follower." And "Embrace the work."

For my wife and other close friends: "We have to learn how to tell people what they need to know, but in a way they can receive it. We have to learn how to step on their shoes without them losing their shine."

In meetings: "You are who you are because of what you were when" or "A system is powerfully designed to get the results it gets."

With close colleagues talking about teamwork: "Two heads are better than one, even if one is a butthead."

As Kent County's administrator, I saw my job as creating ownership and pride among all employees. A great team has ownership from top to bottom, and you don't just get that by paying somebody. You give them the training and resources they need. You listen to their ideas and empower people at every level to make decisions. If you micro-manage their every move, they will not feel trusted or appreciated. When employees take ownership of their work, they give it their best attention and effort. They accept accountability for the outcome of their assignments. And they feel emboldened to improve processes, come up with innovative solutions and drive change.

Within teams, it's important to allow individuals to contribute their own strengths and to improvise, as long as everyone shares a common vision. But some employees may disrupt team harmony by focusing more on gaining personal accolades and advancement. Others may cause conflict or fail to perform. I learned that I must be willing to confront bad behavior in my team and deal with the negative actions and selfish motives that come into play. As human beings, we are all flawed. As leaders, we can't be afraid to tell people what they need to hear in order to make improvement, but we must do it in a way that they will receive the message and try to alter their behavior. The goal is to help the situation, not hurt it.

Every human being wants to be treated fairly and to feel valued. No employee gives their all to an organization without feeling valued and supported. There have been times in my career when I felt that bosses didn't appreciate my experience and knowledge because I was an African American.

At a Kent County leadership workshop, I was one of the people selected to give my perspective on inclusionary leadership. We were asked to share with supervisors and managers some strategies, tips or techniques that we had successfully used to advance diversity and maximize employees' potential by including them. The class was well attended by a diverse group of leadership from all departments of the county. Here are a few key attributes I shared that an inclusive leader demonstrates:

    Listens to others
    Validates the person or staff
    Encourages positive relationships
    Takes advantage of opportunities to help others
    Values diversity
    Gives credit where it is due
    Inspires others to greatness
    Is tolerant of others
    Relies on staff and encourages risk-taking
    Solicits staff input

I am comfortable in leading others and challenging them to believe that they have the capacity and ability to make change happen. I am confident they can thrive and be successful. If you can get the right people on the bus and the wrong people off the bus, you can work together to solve any problem.

We underestimate our capacity to make a difference. We can accomplish great things if hearts and minds are joined together with a common focus.

We have the power to make change happen and build a better world. We just need to use it.

ᴗ CHAPTER 16 ᴗ

Fulfilling the Dream

*"I have a dream that one day this nation will rise up
and live out the true meaning of its creed:
We hold these truths to be self-evident,
that all men are created equal."*
— MARTIN LUTHER KING JR.

D
r. King's "I Have a Dream" address is one of the most famous speeches in American history. The civil rights leader, who was also a Baptist minister, delivered it on August 28, 1963, during the March on Washington for Jobs and Freedom. Standing in front of the Lincoln Memorial, King powerfully expressed the hope for equal opportunity for all people and an end to racial discrimination.

More than a half century later, the dream has not completely come true. There are far too many children growing up in poverty, putting them at a disadvantage from the start. They are hampered by poor nutrition, inadequate health care and housing insecurity. They often attend schools that are lacking in resources compared with schools in more affluent areas. They have fewer opportunities for the kind of out-of-school experiential learning that helps them think independently, improve their confidence and develop leadership traits. These deterrents apply to poor children of all races, but minorities are disproportionately represented. For far too many, the dream remains deferred.

I retired from my job as administrator of Kent County on July 24, 2021. But I did not relinquish my mission of serving others, especially the young people who represent the future of our society. I believe lifting children out of poverty is the best investment we can make for America. We are only as strong as our weakest link.

I grew up poor myself. If not for the people who gave me a hand up when I needed it, I never would have risen to the leadership positions I attained. And so, I feel compelled to create positive opportunities for those growing up today in challenging circumstances. Serving the vulnerable and underserved in our community is what I believe I'm called to do. When I was still in grade school in Smithfield, North Carolina, the Boy Scouts provided my first opportunity to really expand my horizons when I was selected to go away to a camp. By the time I left camp, I was different. I dared to dream. I believed that opportunities would come for me. I began to see myself going to college with a bigger, brighter future ahead.

The Boy Scouts fired up my dreams, and gave me aspiration to begin the task of fulfilling them. I have been involved with many community and charitable groups, but the Boy Scouts will always have a special place in my heart. There have been troubling accusations and lawsuits because of some bad apples that were involved with the organization. But I also know that the Boy Scouts have had a positive impact on many, many lives.

Scouting helps to prepare youth for life. And more importantly, it can prepare them to lead.

Scouts are less likely to commit a crime, and more likely to excel in academics—and 88% less likely to drop out of high school.

Scouts are twice as likely to be a supervisor or leader in their professional life.

Scouts are four times more likely to become an FBI agent.

Scouts are three times more likely to be an astronaut.

Scouts are twice as likely to graduate as an officer from one of our three military academies.

It is clear that scouting grows confidence and builds character. You learn teamwork and how to enlist the help of others to get things done. Scouting helped motivate me to seek opportunity to thrive, even when the odds were stacked against me. It gave me the fertile ground I needed to bloom and flourish.

Dr. King and Whitney M. Young Jr., a civil rights leader who headed the National Urban League, were scouts. However, African Americans have traditionally been underrepresented. Scouting tends to be a legacy organization—a tradition passed down from one generation to another, and this legacy was strongest in the white community. This situation struck me when I went to an annual banquet for the Gerald R. Ford Council of the Boy Scouts. Not one African American was on the podium where Eagle Scouts were honored. That was the beginning point of my commitment to writing a new narrative.

Along with Bill Hardiman, former state senator, I was asked to be co-vice president of Scoutreach, a program designed to raise funds for inner-city and other disadvantaged young people to become exposed to the character development and leadership training of Boy Scouts. Our council's Scoutreach provided after-school and summer programs at no cost for thousands of western Michigan kids each year.

In 2004, I pitched the idea to our Scoutreach Committee of hosting an annual golf outing to raise funds so that at-risk youth could participate in scouting. I even envisioned one day of having fellow North Carolina native Michael Jordan coming and participating with us. The generosity of golfers, sponsors and individuals helped us pay the costs of providing these youngsters with program supplies, registration fees, staff support, field trips to camp and insurance.

Dinah and I established a scholarship fund for needy young people to participate in Adventure Point programs, including overnight stays at the Britt Family Yurt Village.

I eventually was asked to serve a term as president of the Ford Council, becoming the first Black person to hold that position. In 2012, our council merged with eight others in Michigan's Lower Peninsula to form the larger Michigan Crossroads Council.

One of the Ford Council's outstanding recent initiatives is Adventure Point located at the DeVos Family Center for Scouting, northwest of Grand Rapids in Walker, Michigan. Adventure Point emphasizes team building, sustainability, leadership, outdoor adventure and STEM (Science, Technology, Engineering and Math) learning. One of the unique aspects of the site is the Britt Family Yurt Village which provides overnight camping experience for youth. And in 2019, my wife and I established the Wayman and Dinah Britt Adventure Point Scholarship Fund to give more young people access to the leadership and life skills that can be gained there.

As I approached my retirement date of July 24, 2021, I decided that doing something for the community I served was more important than a big party. I enjoy golfing with my friends, and so I thought we could build on the annual Boy Scouts event to benefit them and other nonprofit organizations that are mentoring young people, including the Boys and Girls Club, STEM Greenhouse, the YMCA, Better Wiser Stronger and Meaning in Colors. Each of these entities is dedicated to engaging people in positive action and propelling our youth and community into a better future.

I wanted the event to be about something more than just me, and to go beyond fundraising for a good cause. It needed to be about connecting and inspiring people. It had to be about releasing people from whatever baggage was holding them back from developing positive, inclusive relationships. With the help of friends, business leaders and others in the community, we established the Fulfilling the Dream Celebrity Open that was held over three days to help young people of color get support they need to build their confidence and capacity to succeed. As part of this overall goal, we provided an environment for a diverse group of people to grow their relationships to help achieve this worthy cause.

The three-day event started with a reception on Sunday evening, September 26, 2021 where we recognized community leaders Hattie Patterson, Dan and Betty Groce, Don and Mary Williams and renowned American realist painter Paul Collins and his wife Carol. Monday was a beautiful day for golf at the Egypt Valley Golf Club in Ada Township, just east of Grand Rapids. More than 200 people showed up, including many business and community leaders. And some of my former Michigan teammates came to show their support, namely Campy Russell, Phil Hubbard, Steve Grote, C.J. Kupec and Tim Kuzma, plus former Detroit Piston Walker D. Russell.

I find that recreational activities, such as playing golf together, are fun and effective ways to foster relationships. These shared experiences are an important step in building the trust required to cooperate in solving tough issues. The NIA Centre of Grand Rapids, an African American cultural nonprofit located in Grand Rapids, helped us bring a unique artistic experience to the Open.

The main dinner event held Monday evening also was a social icebreaker, highlighted by the African American company DanceSpire, another local group that displayed unbelievable artistic athleticism. Bill and India Manns were presented the Whitney M. Young Jr. Service Award for their efforts in helping implement opportunities for youth from low-income urban backgrounds. And my longtime friend and prominent local attorney Stephen R. Drew dedicated a scholarship endowment in the name of his father Richard "Dickie" Drew to help young African American males access leadership programs at Adventure Point.

The connection-building continued the final morning when we held a Business Leaders' Summit sponsored by Steelcase in partnership with the Michigan Minority Supplier Development Council (MMSDC). It was a hybrid event with only the speaker and panelists participating in person and attendees taking part virtually because of Covid concerns. During our time together we addressed a report sanctioned by the MMSDC which assesses the growth rate of minority business enterprises and what it would take to close the revenue parity gap. Our keynote speaker, Michelle Sourie Robinson, MMSDC president talked about the disparities in business opportunities for minority small business development and the fact that at the current rate of growth it would take 330 years for minority owned businesses in the United States to reach revenue parity. This projection is untenable and it will take bold steps to change this trajectory.

The Fulfilling the Dream Celebrity Open raised nearly $300,000 thanks to sponsorships, golf participants and the dinner. That money will help the designated nonprofit organizations provide important mentoring opportunities to develop the potential of young people. I received many comments that the program was very meaningful. And no sooner had the event ended than some sponsors and many people told me they wanted to be a part of the next one.

The scarcest resource in the world today is leadership talent capable of transforming communities and organizations to win in tomorrow's world. The competitive edge will go to those who invest in developing a deep and broad pool of leaders. And the greatest obligation of true leadership is to transfer your gift to the next generation. Leadership success is measured by what happens in your absence. The greatest leader the world has ever known was a servant. Jesus left, but He inspired others to carry his message of service over self to millions around the world.

I doubt that anyone looking at the early years of my life would have predicted that I would someday become the administrator of Kent County. Yet somehow I either gravitated into or sought out roles to which I could bring my skills and experiences, as well as my aspiration to serve others. As I look back at my progression through a series of challenges and opportunities, I see how one situation prepared me for the next.

Serving my community taught me a lot. It gave me the ability to further my passion, to grow my capacity to serve others. Ultimately, it was not about me. It was about them. It was about the people. It was about giving young boys and girls hope to fulfill their dreams. Muhammad Ali once said, "Service to others is the rent you pay for being on earth." My role at times was a thankless job. Criticism would sometimes come with decisions I made, but I tried to always do what I believed was in the best interest of the county—and by extension the people's best interest.

Public service is both a calling and a minefield of blame, particularly in divisive and difficult times. No matter what, I tried to demonstrate pride, poise and a commitment to excellence. I will miss my team and the satisfaction that came from getting results. And I look forward to continuing to find ways to help others to fulfill their dreams.

My goal was to build an atmosphere that better served others. I sought to improve our organization—our processes, our culture and our capacity to help people reach their full potential. That was what operational excellence was about—to help bring out the best in people. To unleash their potential.

Running your race in life is not about beating people. It is about releasing your gift to help people in our world.

America as a whole enjoys great prosperity, but we need leaders who are creating an environment in which more of the community can benefit. Income inequality in the country has grown substantially over recent decades, and the Black-White income gap is persistent. Over the course of 17 years working for Kent County, I saw the disparities and inequities that exist in the number of people affected by poverty.

Consider that by 2045, minority groups collectively will represent a majority of the population. Where will our society be if we don't find a way to lift all boats? We have to change the narrative so that diverse community members become the next generation of leaders who build businesses and organizations, and create innovations that move us forward. There is enormous work to do regarding economic inequality, the cost of education, and healing our political divisions. We need positive role models to help expose our youth to new careers and to help build character and leadership skills in them so that they can help us solve these vexing problems.

I am grateful to God that I found my purpose of serving others. Although I retired as county administrator, I have developed relationships that will allow me to continue to help today's young people find their own purpose in life. My dream growing up as a kid on tobacco road was to one day go to a major college and play basketball. That dream has been more than fulfilled. How do we make it possible for every kid across America to fulfill his or her dream?

Martin Luther King came on the scene in a critical window of time. He became a lightning rod for significant change. There are times in history where this happens. When the time is right, people become agitated enough to unite for a higher motive than mere political gain, to sacrifice their lives and to embrace each other long enough to make dreams come true. The question is, what are we willing to sacrifice and how long are we willing to embrace each other for more dreams to come true?

Dr. King and the people in his era sacrificed a lot—and even risked their lives—to make dreams come true. His courage and passion inspired people to come together for a better society. Our country had to give up its old way of thinking and let his voice be heard to get on a better path for justice. And that needs to happen again for more of our youth to fulfill their dreams. We have got to come together; we've got to work together.

Our collective voice needs to rise again. We must have faith that we can make a difference. I believe it can happen. And the time is now.

ACKNOWLEDGMENTS

No man is an island. And what I was able to accomplish in life wouldn't have been possible without many people, some deceased, who helped me along the way.

This book never would have been brought to fruition were it not for my newfound friend at MB Communications, Bill Haney, who helped me to solidify the idea of this book. I was introduced to Bill after coming across one of the many books he has edited or published, *Pigeons, Bloody Noses and Little Skinny Kids: A Story of Wolverine Basketball* by Jeff Mortimer. Thanks, Jeff, for introducing to me to Bill. Thanks, Bill, for all of your foresight and wisdom. The time spent sharing stories over lunch with you on your back deck observing nature and watching the Baltimore Orioles frolic off the balcony was a real treat and a pivotal point in my life. I would like to also acknowledge and thank my co-conspirator, collaborator and friend Ray Serafin for his editorial insight and constructive vision. Bill, you were right. Ray is a consummate professional and was the right man for the job. Thanks Ray for your partnership. It has been profound. Jacinta Calcut at Image Graphics & Design, is another key person on our publishing team whose expertise has been invaluable. The quality of the book could not have been accomplished without her exceptional talent.

I want to give a shout out to Chuck Stoddard, my longtime Michigan State University Spartan friend who gave me my first gig in Grand Rapids at Michigan National Bank-Central after my release from the Los Angeles Lakers. Chuck is a wonderful human being and has one of the driest senses of humor I've ever known. Thanks, Chuck, for your support over the years and for asking, "When are you going to write your book?"

Dave Czurak, former writer for the Grand Rapids Business Journal, thanks for your friendship and your coaching on writing a book. It was just what I needed to help me visualize getting it done!

I am forever grateful to my Aunt Alarce, who is gone now, for her love and support, especially after Ma had passed and when life was hitting me so hard. Aunt Alarce played an important part in my life, encouraging me to grow the talents hidden in me as a young boy.

I owe a great deal of gratitude to others who helped me as I grew up in North Carolina, including Bruce Coats, my first basketball coach at Cleveland High School. I am indebted to all my teachers at Short Journey School, especially my fourth grade teacher Mrs. Thelma Wall along with Mrs. Sanders and Mrs. Fuller, who expressed confidence in me and were instrumental in jump-starting my belief that I was capable of being a leader. And to Principal Mrs. Eva J. Cooper, thanks for the example you set and the inspiration you gave me and all the other children at Short Journey to reach for the stars and to believe that anything was possible in life.

I want to say a big thank you to my Flint Northern High School basketball coaches, especially Bill Frieder who helped make it possible for me to take my athletic ability to the next level. And to my college coaches at the University of Michigan, especially Johnny Orr who was a father figure to me and friend long after he left to be the head coach at Iowa State: Thanks, Coach. And here's a shout out to Richard (Bird) Carter, U of M assistant coach and mentor for helping me develop as a person and student athlete during the critical years of college and transitioning into a professional career. And thanks to legendary U of M football coach, Bo Schembechler. Although I never played for him on the football team, the leadership and zeal he displayed to me and other athletes helped us grow into men.

My journey, which is what much of this book is about, would not have been possible without the many clergy friends and pastors that have helped guide me over the years. I want to acknowledge Bishop Dennis McMurray, Pastor Gary Hankins, Fr. Thomas Smith, Reverend John Guest, Bishop William C. Abney and Reverend Jerry Bishop for their prayers, support and encouragement throughout my journey.

I want to express gratitude to my friends who served with me in the early years on various human services and non-profit boards who were instrumental in my transition from private business to public service in local government. There are too many people to name, but I do want to acknowledge my dear friends Evert Vermeer, Joan Krause and Bob Jamo who served with me on the Kent County Human Services Board. Also, a special thank you to my long-time friend Jim Lareau who worked with me at Michigan National Bank-Central and served with me on the Job Corps Community Relations Council. There was never a problem too big for us to handle!

To my former colleagues and mentors at Steelcase, Dan Wiljanen, Paul Pearson, Ellen Burton, Brian Cloyd, Cal Jeter, George Nelson, Dave Perry, Jim Soule, Bruce McClenithan and Tom Allsberry: Thank you for the many lessons learned and for your friendship over the years. You made a lasting impression on me.

There are too many to name, but I do want to express my gratitude to some of the key friends and colleagues that have played important roles in helping to fulfill my dream and in getting things done during my time at Kent County and since my retirement: Mike Jandernoa, John Kennedy, Dan DeVos, Bill Martin, Jim Hackett, Fred Keller, Hank Meijer, Bill Pink, Teresa Weatherall-Neal, Mark Washington, Christina Keller, Doug DeVos, Jim Keane, Rick Keyes, Rob Casalou, Tina Freese-Decker, Dave & Carol Van Andel, Doug Meijer, and Dick DeVos.

Thank you to my close Scouting friends and golfing buddies: Daniel Groce, Nevin Groce, Floyd Wilson, Stephen Drew, Pat Miles Jr., Walker D. Russell, Kenny McCarty, C.J. Kupec, Tim Kuzma, Aaron Gach, Paul Kelly, Chris Edgar, Bruce Young, Jon Goad, Rich Maike, Don Williams, Nate Moody, Ginny Seyferth, Greg Meyer, Michael Melinn and Ross Melinn for all you have done to help make the Fulfilling the Dream Celebrity Open a reality. And to my special alumni friends and loyalists from the University of Michigan, John U. Bacon, Ron Koehler, Bruce Courtade, Tim Williams and Becky Bechler: Thanks for your friendship and for all you've done to help me! Go Blue!

Also, thank you Carol Paine McGovern, Matthew VanZetten, Diana Sieger and Ron Koehler for all of your sacrifices, support and friendship and all you've done to make Kent Schools Services Network the wonderful success it is in helping to make young dreams come true. You make this world a better place.

To my past and present Kent County Board of Commissioners friends and colleagues: I appreciate your support and the confidence you showed in me over the years. And special thanks to my friend and comrade Jim Day, who always encouraged the "Britter" in me: I could never have done it without you. I am grateful for your loyal support and friendship "Jimmie O'Day."

To my team in Kent County Administration: We accomplished a lot together and without your incredible sacrifices and hard work it never would have been possible. I want to acknowledge my inner circle in Kent County Administration that supported me as county administrator: Jim Day, Matthew VanZetten, Sherry Hall, MaryBeth VanTill, Adam London, Jennifer Headrick, Sandra Winchester, Sandra Ghosten Jones, Pam VanKeuren, Lori Latham, Linda Howell, Matt Woolford, Al Jano, Stephen Duarte, Jeff Dood, Marvin VanNortwick, Amy Rollston, Tim Beck, Sangeeta Ghosh, Craig Paull, Hillary Arthur, Matt Channing, Jenny James, Paul Petr, Teresa Branson, Mike Fortman and Sanda Vazgec. Thank you for your dedication and your teamwork. You are incredible!

Thank you to my brothers, Jay, Jimmy, Curt, Alonza, and my sister Cookie for all your love and support. Jay and Jimmy, thank you for always being there and helping me remember the most important things I needed to share in this book. And to my long-time friend and teammate Campy Russell: Thank you for our many calls and for helping me stay true to myself. This book would have been impossible without your friendship and encouragement. Much respect!

To my cousins Cliff, Sammy, Lillian and Jerry, thanks for the needed help in gathering early family photos that brought back so many fond memories. And to Roger Stanley, my childhood friend, and teammate Timmy Clifton at Cleveland High School: Thank you for your help in securing photos of my early years in North Carolina and for being good friends all these years.

Finally, I want to give special thanks to my sons Eric and Ron, and my daughters, Raven, Desirae, Tia, Ean and Ariel. I love you all! And excuse me while I give another huge shout out to my wife and companion, Dinah. Your patience, love and support has meant so much to me in my journey. Thank you for your keen insights on *Fulfilling the Dream*. I love you!